# Voices from the Edge of Eternity

# VOICES from the Edge of Eternity

Compiled by John MYERS

All Scripture quotations are taken from the King James Version of the Holy Bible.

**Voices from the Edge of Eternity**

John Myers
P.O. Box 30953
Clarksville, TN 37040

ISBN: 978-1-60374-503-1
Printed in the United States of America


Whitaker House
1030 Hunt Valley Circle
New Kensington, PA 15068
www.whitakerhouse.com

**Library of Congress Cataloging-in-Publication Data**

Voices from the edge of eternity / compiled By John Myers.
p. cm.
Summary: "A compilation of the words and experiences of people both famous and obscure just before death—including such figures as Luther, Darwin, Napoleon, and many more—reveals the remarkable agreement of their testimonies and the light that each account sheds on the life that awaits us after death"—Provided by publisher.
ISBN 978-1-60374-503-1 (trade pbk. : alk. paper) 1. Last words. I. Myers, John, 1925–
BR1702.M9 2012
236'.2—dc23
2012014115



1 2 3 4 5 6 7 8 9 10 11 19 18 17 16 15 14 13 12

# Contents

# Preface

Death is a subject no one can treat lightly. It is too *final* for that. Beauty, honor, wealth, earthly power, hopes, and dreams—all are swallowed up in that finality. Man is born with his hands clenched; he dies with them wide open. Entering life, he desires to grasp everything; leaving the world, all that he possessed has slipped away.

But it is not so much death itself as it is the mystery of what lies beyond that closed door that has haunted mankind since time immemorial. Seemingly, there is no tangible answer to this mystery—or is there?

Several years ago, I was impressed with the striking glimpses into eternity afforded by several accounts I read, here and there, of deathbed testimonies. Then, one day, I stumbled across an old book—published in 1898—that contained scores of such testimonies. I was amazed and deeply shaken. Here was a cross section of people from every walk of life—young and old, saint and sinner—who, just before leaving this life, saw quite clearly beyond the grave. Their testimonies were sharp and clear, and all bore witness to the same essential facts.

From that hour, I knew I would compile this book. It took me nearly ten years to finish it. The final result is far from exhaustive, but I believe it constitutes convincing evidence that God has, again and again, answered man's fateful question concerning eternity.

A book of this nature is essentially history and, as such, is dependent on the records of the past. Aside from the contemporary, and some older, testimonies gleaned from here and there, I am indebted primarily to three books published in the nineteenth century: *The Dying Hours of Good and Bad Men Contrasted* by D. P. Kidder, published in 1848 by Carlton and Phillips of New York; *Selections from Testimonies and Dying Words of Saints and Sinners* by A. H. Gottschall, published in 1898 by the author in Harrisburg, Pennsylvania; and *Dying Testimonies of the Saved and Unsaved* by S. B. Shaw, published in 1898 by the author in the United States. It is this last book that served as my original inspiration and basis for the compilation of this present volume.

In my search for choice subject matter, I have deleted more than I have retained, especially with regard to the testimonies found in the above mentioned books. Also, in many cases, I have condensed and adapted the text in order to get to the essential message conveyed. In such editing, however, I have in no way tampered with the authors' meaning or import. I have tried to preserve the colloquial expressions current to that time in history, as well as the authors' doctrinal outlooks.

The testimony of this book is that thousands of men and women—unbelievers, as well as believers—standing on the very edge of eternity, caught up in life's most dramatic experience, have seen quite clearly beyond the grave. What they saw and sensed not only bears evidence as to the fact of man's immortality, but it also answers many pertinent questions that perplex the minds of thinking people today. I refer to such questions as the accuracy of the biblical accounts of life after death, the truth or fallacy of reincarnation, and so forth.

Far more important than a mere collection of scientific evidence, to many, this book will constitute the dawn of what the prophets of old called *hope,* that glorious sense of goal and destiny that alone can defy the death grip of materialism that threatens to plunge our generation into the madness of a purposeless life.

It is to that word *hope,* and all its treasures for the human heart, that I dedicate these pages.

—John Myers

*O death, where is thy sting? O grave, where is thy victory?*

—1 Corinthians 15:55

# David Appleby
# (1923)

*Submitted by his widow, Rosalee Mills Appleby, of Canton, Mississippi*

If I lived a thousand years, I would not forget that September morning of 1924 when we boarded a ship in New York Harbor bound for Brazil as Christ's messengers. Our wedding had occurred just seven weeks prior, and life was radiant with promise. The image in our hearts of our homeland was the America of Woodrow Wilson. From the deck, we watched the Statue of Liberty shrink into the distant horizon.

After eleven days of blue above and below, we sailed into the bay of the world's most beautiful city, Rio de Janeiro. During the next ten months, we studied the Portuguese language in this charming place.

Our place of service was to be in the interior of the giant state of Minas Gerais. We were invited to remain in the capital city, Belo Horizonte, until after the birth of our baby. Our plan was to go into Brazil's interior immediately after this anticipated event.

During the days of waiting, David had a checkup that revealed the necessity of an operation for a stomach ulcer. Our physician marked the first anniversary of our arrival in Brazil as the time for surgery in the local hospital.

A beloved missionary couple, Mr. and Mrs. J. R. Allen, stayed with David. Mrs. Allen had training as a nurse, and they both were tireless in their loving care throughout the six days he survived the operation. A copy of a letter that Mrs. Allen wrote my family will describe David's witness.

> About two-thirty a.m., David began saying, "They are calling, calling, calling—there, in heaven!" Then, for an hour, he sang and talked about heaven. I had heard of people having a vision like this but had never witnessed it. It was the most beautiful thing I have ever seen.

On one occasion, he said, "I didn't know it could be so beautiful. All is well with my soul!" We stayed by him until he went to that place where there will be no more pain. His life and influence here have been, and will be, a blessing to all those with whom he came into contact.

It has been a source of thanksgiving to God that I could be with my husband during his last hours. His body was still in the adjoining room at dawn when our son came. During that long, long night, doubt crept in. I looked up into my Savior's face and asked Him if I had run unsent, mistaken in the call I had been so sure of before. Into my heart came the assurance that all was well and that Jesus was at the helm of everything.

**Compiler's Note:** As I read this account, I was reminded of the verse "*Verily, verily, I say unto you, except a corn of wheat fall into the ground and die, it abideth alone: but if it die, it bringeth forth much fruit*" (John 12:24). This touching scene was not the end but rather the beginning of something much more glorious than could have been had it not occurred. Truly, our "*times are in thy hand*" (Psalm 31:15). Not only did the young husband receive a glorious entrance into his heavenly reward, but also from that desperately lonely night of childbirth, so full of sorrow, pain, and doubt—with her lover's body lying in the very next room—Rosalee Appleby (1885–1991) rose to become one of the great missionaries to Brazil, spending nearly forty years in that needy land from 1924 to 1960.

My correspondence with "Miss Appleby" revealed her to be not only a woman of indefatigable spirit with keen insight into the richest truths of God's Word, but also—and more important—a woman of prayer.

Who can say that the unprecedented spiritual growth recorded today in the nation of Brazil has not come out of the tears of Rosalee Appleby's prayers and those of others like her? And who can say that these precious tears of intercession would ever have been sown if she had not first sown those tears of earthly sorrow and loneliness as a bright young girl giving birth to a fatherless baby and facing a difficult future alone in a strange land?

# Voltaire (1778)

When Voltaire felt the stroke, which he realized must terminate in death, he was overpowered with remorse. At once, he sent for the priest, wanting to be "reconciled to the church." His infidel flatterers hastened to his chamber to prevent his recantation, but it was only to witness his ignominy and their own. He cursed them to their faces and, since his distress was increased by their presence, repeatedly and loudly exclaimed, "Begone! It is you that have brought me to my present condition. Leave me, I say—begone! What a wretched glory is this which you have produced for me!"

Hoping to allay his anguish by a written recantation, he had it prepared, signed it, and saw it witnessed. But it was unavailing. For two months, he was tortured with such an agony as led him at times to gnash his teeth in impotent rage against God and man. At other times, in plaintive accents, he would plead, "O Christ! O Lord Jesus!" Then, turning his face, he would cry out, "I must die—abandoned of God and of men!"

As his end drew near, his condition became so frightful that his infidel associates were afraid to approach his bedside. Still, they guarded the door so that others might not see how awfully an infidel was compelled to die. Even his nurse repeatedly said that for all the wealth of Europe, she would never see another infidel die. It was a scene of horror that lies beyond all exaggeration.

Such is the well-attested end of this man who had a natural sovereignty of intellect, excellent education, great wealth, and much earthly honor.

— Edward Davies, *The Contrast Between Infidelity and Christianity, as Seen in Death-bed Testimonies* (1879)

# Dwight L. Moody (1899)

To the world, December 22 was the shortest day of the year. For Dwight L. Moody, its dawn in 1899 ushered in a day that knew no night. For forty-four years, Moody had been a partaker of the divine life, and the transition from the visible to the unseen—from the sphere of the temporal to the eternal—was no interruption in his life. In other realms, he continued to serve the same Master whose cause he loved with devotion and served with tireless energy.

Within a few hours of the end, Moody shared with the family his conviction that he was improving. The day before, he had seemed rather more nervous than usual but spoke cheerfully about himself. In reply to an inquiry about his level of comfort, he had said, "Oh, yes! God is very good to me—and so is my family." Rare was the man who loved his family as much or who worked as devotedly. Frequently, he had been heard to say, "Life is very sweet to me, and there is no position of power or wealth that could tempt me from the throne God has given me." Perhaps it was the fact that he was not tired of life or of serving God that made him so ready to leave, for he knew the joy of Christian service as few have experienced it.

The final summons came without warning. During the first half of the night, his son-in-law, A. P. Fitt, had been at his bedside. Moody slept the greater part of the time. At three in the morning, his son W. R. (Will) Moody, came to his bedside. For several hours, the patient was restless and unable to sleep. By around six in the morning, however, he became quiet and fell into a natural sleep.

He awoke about an hour later. His son heard him speaking in slow and measured words, "Earth recedes; heaven opens before me."

His son's first impulse was to try to arouse him from what must have been a dream.

"No, this is no dream, Will," he said. "It is beautiful! It is like a trance! If this is death, it is sweet! There is no valley here! God is calling me, and I must go!"

Meanwhile, the nurse was summoning the family and the physician, who had spent the night in the house. Mr. Moody continued to talk quietly and seemed to be voicing his last messages to the loved ones he was leaving.

"I have always been an ambitious man," he said. "Not ambitious to leave wealth or possessions but to leave lots of work for you to do. You will carry on Mount Hermon. Paul will take up the seminary when he is older. Fitt will look after the institute. And Ambert [a nephew] will help you all in the business details."

Then, it seemed as though he saw beyond the veil, for he exclaimed, "This is my triumph; this is my coronation day! I have been looking forward to it for years."

With this, his face lit up, and he said in a voice of joyful rapture, "Dwight! Irene! I see the children's faces." (This referred to his two grandchildren, whom God had taken home within the past year.)

With this, he became unconscious. Until this time, no drugs whatsoever had been administered. In half an hour, however, he revived under the effect of heart stimulants, and, as he regained consciousness, he feebly uttered these words: "No pain! No valley!" Rallying further, he added, "If this is death, it's not bad at all! It's sweet!"

Later, raising himself on his elbow, he exclaimed, "What does all this mean? What are you all doing here?"

His wife explained that he had not been well, and, immediately, it all seemed to be clear to him. Then, he said, "This is a strange thing! I've been beyond the gates of death to the very portals of heaven. And here I am, back again. It is very strange!"

A little later, he said, "This is my coronation day! It's glorious!" Then he talked about the work he was leaving behind, assigning to his two sons the Northfield schools and, to his daughter and her husband, the Chicago Bible Institute. Asked what his wife's charge would be, he said, "Oh, Mama is like Eve, the mother of us all!"

To the urgent plea that he remain with his family, he said, "I'm not going to throw my life away. I'll stay as long as God wants me to; but if my time is come, I'm ready."

Something was soon said that showed how clear his mind was, for he remarked with deliberation, "This is the twenty-second of December, isn't it? Five months ago today, Irene died, and in this room."

It was actually only four months, but anyone might have made such a mistake.

To the very last, he was thinking of those around him. Turning to his wife only a little while before he left, he said, "This is terrible on you, Mama; it's such a shock. I'm sorry to distress you in this way. Brace yourself. It is hard to be kept in such anxiety."

A few minutes before noon, he was evidently sinking once again, and, as the doctor approached to administer another hypodermic injection of nitroglycerine, Mr. Moody looked at him in a questioning way and said, "Doctor, I don't know about this. Do you think it wise?"

The doctor said he thought the injection would be all right.

"Well," Mr. Moody said, "it's prolonging the agony for the family!"

The doctor turned away, seeing that the patient's life could not be saved. In a few moments, another sinking turn came on, and from it Mr. Moody awoke in the presence of Him whom he loved and had served so long and faithfully.

It was not like death, for he fell asleep quietly and peacefully, and it was not hard to imagine his reception in that other world among the host of loved ones awaiting his coming. The whole occurrence was such, in the mercy of God, that the *substance* as well as the sting of death was removed.

—Arthur Percy Fitt, *The Shorter Life of D. L. Moody* (1900)

# Little Willie Leonard Sees Jesus (1881)

The following account of the death of Willie Leonard, only six years old, will be of added interest to anyone who may have read a book written by Anna Leonard, *One Year with Jesus*. It is taken from a letter written by Willie's mother at the time of his death in 1881.

One day about two weeks before Willie died, he came in from his play and said, "Mama, it seems to me I wouldn't want to die." When asked why, he said, "Oh, I wouldn't want to leave you folks here. But then, I suppose I would be very happy in heaven. And, Mama, I would watch over you."

His mother clasped him in her arms. She loved him very much, yet somehow she felt that the angels were beckoning to him. She talked with him of the joys that awaited him in heaven and of how the angels would meet him there.

Willie replied, "Mama, I don't want any little lamb on my tombstone. I want a little boy lying on the grass as you have seen me lie in the summertime when I was tired out with play." (He had never seen or heard of anything of the kind, but such a stone now marks his grave.)

The premonition proved true, for he soon took sick with scarlet fever of a diphtherial form and lived but two days.

He was such a patient little sufferer through it all! When asked if he was not a pretty sick little boy, he replied, "No, not very sick, but I think Jesus is going to take me to heaven to live." As he spoke, an angelic look of holy rapture and a radiant smile came over his face. His father was called, and as he talked with him about it, that same glorious smile again illuminated his face. He then talked about the disposal of his toys, books, Sunday school cards, and papers.

He spoke of a new hat, which he said he would not need now, and his mother talked with him of the beautiful crown awaiting him in heaven, although her heart seemed bursting with grief.

"Willie," said she, "no one can see Jesus when He comes except the one He comes after, so when you see Him will you tell me?"

"Yes," he replied, "if I can talk. If not, I will point to Him."

When his little brother told him that his father had gone to get the doctor, Willie said, "Oh, I would rather that Jesus would take me to heaven than for Dr. Taplin to make me well!"

In a few hours, he was quite restless and delirious. I now quote from the letter verbatim:

> As we laid him back on his pillow, his eyes remained wide open and fixed. We felt his feet and found them to be cold. I hastened and warmed flannels and wrapped them. We chafed his hands, although his

fingernails were blue. How could we believe that our Willie was dying?—Willie, our hope, our pride, the joy of our home. But so it was, and as we gathered round his bed, we wept as only parents can weep at such times and talked loving words to his inanimate form.

He was lying very still when all at once one little hand was raised, and he pointed upward for a moment as his dear lips moved in an effort to speak.

"'Willie," I cried aloud, "do you see Jesus?"

His hand was laid again by his side; he breathed shorter and less frequently a few times and then ceased forever. In his last moments, he had remembered the signal agreed upon between him and me and he had pointed to Jesus.

When the body that was so beautiful and dear to us was lowered into the silent grave, and the earth fell with a hollow sound upon the box below, it seemed as if I could not rise above the shock.

Then I felt, as it were, a light breath fan my cheek, and a sweet voice seemed to say, "Mama, I am not there; don't cry. I am happy!" My tears dried in an instant, and I cannot now think of him as anywhere but in that beautiful heaven where he longed to go.

—S. B. Shaw, *Dying Testimonies of Saved and Unsaved* (1898)

# The Advice of Ethan Allen, Noted Infidel, to His Dying Daughter

Ethan Allen was a professed infidel and the author of a book against the divinity of Jesus Christ. His wife was a Christian—earnest, cheerful, and devoted. She died an early death, leaving behind an only daughter, who soon became the idol of her father. The fragile, sensitive child entwined herself about the knotty and gnarled limbs of the oak. Before long, however, tuberculosis marked this fair girl for its own, and she gradually wasted away, until the sight of her was enough to bring tears to the hardest heart.

One day, her father came into her room and, sitting beside her bedside, took her wan little hand in his. She looked up into his face and said, "My dear father, I'm going to die."

"Oh no, my child. No!" Allen replied. "The spring is coming, and with the birds and breezes and the bloom, your pale cheeks will blush with health."

"The doctor was here today," she continued. "I felt I was nearing the grave, and I asked him to tell me plainly what I had to expect. I told him that it was a great thing to exchange worlds and that I did not wish to be deceived about myself. If I was going to die, I had some preparations I wanted to make. He then told me my disease is beyond human skill. You will bury me by the side of mother, for that was her dying request. But, Father, you and Mother did not agree on religion. Mother often spoke to me of the blessed Savior, who died for us all. She used to pray for both you and me, that the Savior might be our Friend and that we might all see Him as our Savior when He sits enthroned in His glory."

Her eyes looked desperately into his, and she said, "I don't feel that I can go alone through the dark valley of the shadow of death. Tell me, Father, whom shall I follow: you or Mother? Shall I reject Christ, as you have taught me, or shall I accept Him? He was Mother's Friend in the hour of her great sorrow."

There was an honest heart beneath that rough exterior. Though tears nearly choked his utterances, the old soldier said, "My child, cling to your mother's Savior. She was right. I'll try to follow you to that blessed place."

A serene smile overspread the face of the dying girl, and who can doubt there is an unbroken family in heaven?

—Shaw, *Dying Testimonies of Saved and Unsaved*

# Anne Boleyn (1536)

Anne Boleyn, the second wife of Henry VIII of England, was beheaded at the instigation of her husband, who, the day after her death, married Jane Seymour. The charge brought against her was adultery, but it was never proven.

Four others were beheaded with her, one of whom was Norris, a faithful and virtuous servant. He was promised his life if he would accuse Boleyn, but, instead, he declared that she was innocent and that he would die a thousand deaths rather than defame her. The three others who were executed also vindicated her to the last. So little respect was paid to her body that, with brutal insolence, it was put into a crude chest that was made for sending arrows to Ireland.

To those sent to lead her to execution, she said, "Commend me to the king, and tell him he is constant in his course of advancing me. From a private gentlewoman, he made me a marchioness, and from a marchioness, a queen. Now, having no higher degree of earthly honor left to offer, he hath made me a martyr."

Then she was heard to say, "I hear say the executioner is very good, and I have a little neck. To Christ I commend my soul."

—A. H. Gottschall, *Selections from Testimonies and Dying Words of Saints and Sinners*, (1898)

# Saved Just in Time

Alice's life had always been a sad one—at least, as far as she could remember. Perhaps, her first three years of infancy had been as pleasant and happy as if she had been born in a more comfortable home, but Alice couldn't be sure about it, and no one else could speak for her. Certainly, she had experienced misery and unhappiness for most of her adolescent life.

Shortly after her third birthday, some strange men, all dressed in black, came to her house and took away a long, dark box, and Alice never saw her mother again. Although she couldn't remember much about that day, it represented a big, black spot that seemed to block all the sunlight from life. From that day on, life became hard for Alice, now the youngest of five motherless children no longer subject to the care and nurturing that only a mother can provide. With a home atmosphere full of such moral degradation, it is a wonder that she did not fall deeper into a life of sin. Two of her sisters lived openly sinful lives, and assuredly, the brother whom she lived with and for whom she kept house was no better.

One day, a companion of Alice's brother came to the house. When he finally went away, he left behind a girl of seventeen with a burden of shame, sorrow, and disgrace that she felt she could not bear. Alice went to her two sisters—the only people in the world who could stand in the place of a mother's love—to seek comfort.

"Nonsense!" her sister Kate said. "Why, you'll get used to it!"

Her other sister, Bettina, though a little more sympathetic, was even more discouraging. "I never thought you'd feel like that," she said. "But it's too late to mend matters now. It could have been helped yesterday but not today; what's done can't be undone. There isn't a respectable woman in the world who'd speak to you now!"

Alice walked away as if in a dream. *What's done can't be undone,* she kept repeating to herself, as if to fasten the dreadful statement upon her mind and memory. Occasionally, the words changed, and she repeated, *It's too late to mend matters now.* It was the old argument used so successfully in thousands of instances, which maintained that one step down the ladder of disgrace involved the entire distance and that there was no hope, no way of escape, after the first wrongdoing.

*There's no help for it; you are doomed now.*

*You might as well take what pleasure you can out of this life.*

In such cases, someone in Alice's shoes is bound to face matters with a sense of utter hopelessness. A young girl, whose better nature is fighting against the horror of her situation, allows that nature to yield the battle. *It is no use trying to be good,* she concludes despairingly.

So it was with Alice Sawyer. She knew of no one in the village to whom she could go for help or advice, and she quickly gave up her struggle to do right.

*It isn't my fault,* she replied to herself when her semi-dormant conscience spoke out and would be heard. *There simply isn't any way out for me, or if there is, I can't find it—and that's the same thing.*

Weeks passed, during which no one would have suspected that Alice Sawyer felt any repugnance toward the careless, irregular sort of life she was leading.

"There, I knew she'd get used to it soon enough," exclaimed Kate one day.

But Bettina said nothing. Deep down in her heart, there was a sorrow for her youngest sister, but she did not know how to put it into words.

After a time, Alice left home and found her way to Grand Rapids, Michigan, where she began to search for work. Like many others, she imagined that it would be easier to hide her sense of shame in the midst of a crowd. Although she preferred to remain lost, instead, she was found—found by the One who came to seek and to save that which was lost. (See Matthew 18:11; Luke 19:10.)

Near the beginning of her search for work, Alice discovered that at least one part of Kate's disheartening prophecy was untrue. She came across an earnest Christian woman who not only spoke to her but also took Alice into her own home for the night. The next day, this woman brought her to Grand Rapids' Salvation Army Rescue Home. Alice wanted to stay there and was grateful. Yet it all seemed so strange and unexpected that it took her some time to realize that the way out of her sin and misery had been found.

Kneeling by her bedside one night, Alice claimed for herself the power of that uttermost salvation that alone can take away the bitterness from the memories of her painful past and that alone can make it possible to sing,

> He breaks the power of cancelled sin,
> He sets the prisoner free;
> His blood can make the foulest clean;
> His blood availed for me![1]

That night marked an end to Alice's unhappy days—the "black ones," as she sometimes called them in contrast to the "white ones" of her new life. The one sorrow that remained in Alice's heart was for those she left behind, those without

1. Charles Wesley, "O for a Thousand Tongues to Sing," 1739.

any knowledge of Christ. She prayed for them all, especially for her father, who was seventy-one years old by that time.

"It will take something to touch my father's heart," she told the captain of the home, "but I am praying for him, and I believe he will give his heart to God." That "something" that could touch her father's heart came sooner than she may have expected.

Alice soon became ill and was taken to the hospital. After she had been there a short time, it became evident that she would never be able to leave. But she had no fear. Her only sorrow was that she had hoped to be able to go to others with the story of the wonderful salvation that had entered her life. On the first evening of her stay in the hospital, the captain and lieutenant of the Salvation Army rescue home stayed with her for a few hours. As they were saying good night, Alice suddenly dropped on her knees beside the bed. It was a striking picture. On one side were the two Salvationists in their uniforms; on the other side was a nurse in her uniform. Between them knelt a girl of eighteen who had been saved just in time from a life of misery and sorrow. It seemed as if the very light of heaven were striking through, illuminating the scene with divine radiance and blessing. It may indeed have been so, for Alice was nearing the very gates of heaven.

"I do love you, Captain," said Alice. Then, with her eyes fixed on the face of the man who had led her into the light of salvation through Jesus, she passed quietly and peacefully away to that land where there is no more pain, for the "*former things are passed away*" (Revelation 21:4).

This scene itself would have been a beautiful ending to a story that had begun in such sadness and gloom. It was indeed a bright, white, glorious day in Alice's short life, but it did not mark the end of her work on earth.

The "something" that was to touch her father's heart proved to be his youngest daughter's death. At the simple funeral service, he came forward like a child, knelt beside her coffin, and, shaking with sobs, asked God to help him meet his Alice in the great, wonderful land beyond the grave.

—Article from Salvation Army newsletter, *The War Cry*, by Adjutant Elizabeth M. Clark

# Napoleon Bonaparte (1821)

This great emperor of France died in exile. His last recorded words were, "I die before my time, and my body will be given back to the earth to become food for worms. Such is the fate of him who has been called the great Napoleon. What an abyss lies between my deep misery and the eternal kingdom of Christ!"

—Gottschall, *Selections from Testimonies and Dying Words*

# An Elephant Hunt That Opened Heaven

*Submitted by Loren Cunningham, Youth With a Mission, Pasadena, California*

I heard an outstanding testimony from missionary Paul Landrus when I was visiting the nation of Liberia, in western Africa.

Paul, whom I know personally, was in the jungle hunting elephants with an eighteen-year-old African boy. He shot an elephant, but his gun sight was off, and the animal was only wounded. The elephant turned and charged, and though Paul tried to hide behind a tree, the animal reached around the tree with its trunk and began squeezing the life out of him. He took the elephant's snout and began to squeeze it, which somewhat loosened its grip around his midriff, but, by this time, the animal's trumpeting had stirred up a whole herd of elephants that came lumbering through the thick of the jungle. In the providence of God, one of them hit the back end of the wounded elephant, spinning it around and loosening the grip of its trunk. At that moment, the African boy came running out to help

Brother Landrus, but one of the elephants got him. The boy was gored from his groin almost to his throat. As the elephants carried him away, the poor boy was screaming, "Pa, I die! Pa, I die!"

Brother Landrus followed to find where the elephants had taken him, as elephants often bury their prey in shallow graves. Sure enough, these elephants had scraped out a shallow grave and covered the fatally wounded boy with leaves and dirt. Paul uncovered him and, from that moment on, declared that nothing would ever dissuade him that there was a heaven. This African boy, saved out of heathenism for only a short while and not preconditioned to descriptions of heaven, began to describe the angels and spoke of music that Landrus knew he had never heard in his lifetime. In a few moments, the boy was gone, but in those fleeting last moments, he had clearly seen heaven's glory and even heard its glorious sounds.

# Catherine Booth
## (1890)

*Wife of William Booth, founder of the Salvation Army*

The waters are rising, but so am I. I am not going under, but over! Do not be concerned about dying; go on living well, and the dying will be right."

—Gottschall, *Selections from Testimonies and Dying Words*

# King Charles IX of France (1574)

*For this shall every one that is godly pray unto thee in a time when thou mayest be found: surely in the floods of great waters they shall not come nigh unto him.* (Psalm 32:6)

This wicked king's character was a compounded mix of passion, acuteness, heartlessness, and cunning. The infamous massacre of St. Bartholomew, August 24 to October 3, 1572, was the culmination of a series of treacheries toward the Huguenots, French Protestants who had become influenced by the writings of John Calvin. During this period, Catholics killed as many as ten thousand Protestants across the country. These actions greatly disgraced his reign.

On May 30, 1574, while Charles was still a young man of only twenty-four years, death reached forth its awful hand. Its clutch tore away kingly robes, and as the crown that had given him such authority over the lives of men fell from his brow, he slipped into the dark night of eternity, a naked soul.

No doubt, for the sake of a watching world, the Spirit of God opened his eyes to show him what awaited beyond that dark veil. History has recorded the remorse and cry of anguish that followed.

During his last hours, he cried, "Oh, my nurse, my nurse! What blood, what murders, what evil counsels have I followed!" Then, a futile prayer: "Oh, my God, pardon me and have mercy on me if Thou canst. I know what I am. What shall I do? I am lost; I see it well!"

—Shaw, *Dying Testimonies of Saved and Unsaved*

# Lady Jane Grey (1554)

Lady Jane Grey was queen of England for only ten days. Apparently through the uneasiness of Queen Mary, she and her husband were beheaded on the same day.

From the platform, she addressed the bystanders and there, committing herself to God. Her beautiful throat was then bared, and, after tying a handkerchief over her eyes and feeling for the block, she laid her head upon it.

Before the axe fell, she exclaimed, "Lord, into Thy hands I commend my spirit!"

—Gottschall, *Selections from Testimonies and Dying Words*

# Lt. Masao Nishizawa

*Notorious Japanese War Criminal*

A happy, vivacious young girl set sail for Japan on October 9, 1916. Irene Webster-Smith came from an aristocratic family. Irish to the core, she bubbled over with a delightful wit that sometimes startled the ultra "prim and proper," but she would attract thousands of Japanese to her in later years.

Little did this talented Irish girl realize that, one day, she would be used by God to transform the lives of fourteen of the toughest war criminals in Japan. How did the miracle take place?

Lt. Masao Nishizawa was one of the Japanese military leaders convicted of war crimes after World War II. The International War Crimes Tribunal found him guilty and sentenced him to death by hanging. He was awaiting execution in Tokyo's Sugamo Prison when he first met Miss Webster-Smith.

Nishizawa's wife was a Christian and was deeply concerned about her husband. Allowed to see him for only half an hour each month, she had taken him a copy of the gospel of John during one of her visits. Nishizawa, however, was not interested. Hardened by sins of the deepest dye, he was completely indifferent to his wife's endeavors to bring him to Christ.

One day, Miss Webster-Smith—called *Sensei,* meaning "teacher" or "wise one," by the Japanese people who knew her—went to speak at a women's meeting in Kashiwa. After the meeting, Mrs. Nishizawa introduced herself to Sensei and then pleaded with her to see her husband in prison, saying, "I am deeply concerned about my husband, and I want very much for him to become a Christian before he dies. If only you would go, I would give up my visiting privilege for you."

Such a moving appeal was irresistible, and Sensei promised to do her best. She soon found, however, that Nishizawa and the other war crimes prisoners at Sugamo were held under tight security. The authorities were taking no chances, especially since one prisoner's wife had smuggled poison into the prison while visiting her husband. After she had smeared it on the wire mesh of the interview booth, her husband had licked it off and died.

At first, it seemed impossible for Sensei to break through the regulations and red tape of the prison bureaucracy. But her God-inspired enthusiasm and determination at last convinced the authorities that this charming old lady had a right to see the doomed Nishizawa, and she was admitted into the great gray stone building.

The interview booth was heavily guarded as Sensei sat on one side of the heavy wire mesh that separated her from Nishizawa. After a silent prayer, she said, "I have seen your wife and children, and they are well. I met your wife at a Christian meeting."

"She told me she had been converted," Nishizawa replied, "and she left me a booklet."

The tone of his voice conveyed no interest. But Sensei quickly seized her chance. *The booklet must be the gospel,* she thought. This gave Sensei the golden opportunity of telling the prisoner that the Christ of that book died on the cross for the sins of men and that He would freely pardon all who would truly repent and believe in Him. She went on to explain that Christ would receive such believers into His glorious kingdom, where they would live eternally with Him.

Nishizawa was visibly moved by the earnest and confident preaching of the gospel in that prison booth. Before the interview ended, he asked a vital question: "Do you mean that He could forgive my sins? I have committed terrible sins. You cannot imagine what they are."

Sensei quickly assured Nishizawa that there was hope for the worst sinner who trusts in the cleansing blood of Jesus Christ and believes on Him as his personal Savior.

Deeply moved by the Holy Spirit, the prisoner prayed with Sensei, then and there, crying to God for mercy. Afterward, there came into his heart a peace and a joy he had never known before. Sensei heard him whisper, "Thank God, and thank you."

The great transaction was done! Nishizawa was a new creature in Christ Jesus. (See 2 Corinthians 5:17.) At once, he told Sensei that he believed Christ had saved him. The missionary then urged him to find some person in that prison to tell what Christ had done for him.

The prisoner's only chance was during exercise time, for he was in solitary confinement, and, even then, he was not supposed to talk to the other prisoners. But Nishizawa promised he would do his best to witness for his newly found Savior. This he did with such amazing success that, one by one, thirteen other war criminals were brought to Christ in Sugamo Prison. They asked to be baptized by the Baptist prison chaplain.

Then, one day, there came a deep sense of urgency to Sensei that she must go at once and visit Nishizawa again. But the officials at headquarters were adamant. She had used the one interview permitted; another clemency visit was completely out of the question.

Knowing that the urgent call had come from God, she felt she must, at all costs, see Nishizawa again before he was executed. She marched into the office of the only man in Japan who could open the way for her: General MacArthur, a man who virtually ruled all of Japan at that time.

MacArthur received her courteously and listened to her plea. He then gave her permission to see the prisoner once again, even providing a staff car to drive her to the prison.

In the interview room, she looked keenly at Nishizawa as he was brought in. His face was radiant with joy as he exclaimed, "Only this morning, I asked God to send you to see me. He answered my prayer! I want to give you instructions for the care of my wife and children, and a last message for them and for my parents."

Thus, Sensei and Nishizawa prayed together and said good-bye.

Just before Nishizawa was executed, Sensei received a letter from him. It read:

Mother Smith,

I appreciate you sincerely, and that you saw me again and gave me kind encouragement, sharing your busy time. Thank you also by the name of the Lord with the other brethren, hearing that the favor of baptism was realized by your unusual efforts.

I am living thankful days, believing that I may receive salvation of the Holy Ghost on my last day and, entirely trusting in Him, that for me—saved by the grace of God—"to live is Christ, and to die is gain" (Philippians 1:21).

I pray your good health by the name of the Lord Jesus Christ and God the Father.

Yours sincerely,<br>A saved sinner,<br>M. Nishizawa

Two days later, Sensei learned that Nishizawa and one of the other converts had been executed.

# William Grimshaw (1763)

In his last moments, noted evangelist William Grimshaw, one of the founders of Methodism, was asked how he felt. He replied, "As happy as I can be on earth and as sure of glory as if I were in it. I have nothing to do but to step out of this bed into heaven!"

—Gottschall, *Selections from Testimonies and Dying Words*

# Byron Bunson (1860)

Byron Bunson, born in 1791, was one of the most distinguished statesmen and scholars of Germany. In 1841, he was sent on a special mission to London to negotiate the establishing of an Anglo-Prussian bishopric in Jerusalem. Shortly afterward, he was appointed ambassador at the English court. He is known in literature by many outstanding works, such as *Constitution of the Church of the Future*, *Christianity and Mankind*, and *God in History*. He was a great philosopher.

He died in Bonn, Germany, in 1860. On his deathbed, he cried out, "All bridges that one builds through life fail at such a time as this; nothing remains but the bridge of the Savior!"

—Shaw, *Dying Testimonies of Saved and Unsaved*

# "It Is Easier to Get into Hell than It Will Be to Get Out"

*Submitted by Rev. W. C. Muffit of Cleveland, Ohio*

In the village of Montgomery, Michigan, in the spring of 1884, an infidel—the husband of a spiritualist—was stricken with disease. He had such a hatred for the cause of Christ that he had requested previously that his body not be carried to a church for funeral services, nor any pastor be called upon to officiate.

Now, as he was nearing the shores of eternity, he turned his face toward the wall and began to talk of his future prospects. His wife saw that he was troubled in spirit and endeavored to comfort and console him by telling him not to be afraid. She told him that his spirit would return to her, and they would commune together then, as now. But this gave him no comfort in this awful hour.

With a look of despair, he said, "I see a great high wall rising around me, and I am finding out at last—when it is too late—that it is easier to get into hell than it will be to get out."

A few moments later, his spirit had departed from this world to receive the "reward of unrighteousness." This conversation was heard by my sister-in-law who was present at the time of his death.

—Shaw, *Dying Testimonies of Saved and Unsaved*

# Archibald Campbell (1661)

This man, the 1st Marquess of Argyll, was executed for treason in Edinburgh, Scotland, on May 27, 1661. On the morning of his death, while engaged in settling his worldly business, he was so overpowered with a sense of the divine presence that he broke out in raptures, saying, "I am now ordering my affairs, and God is just now saying to me, 'Son, be of good cheer! Thy sins are forgiven thee.'"

—John Johnstone, *The Scottish Christian Herald* (1841)

# John Hunt (1848)

*Apostle to Fiji*

The Republic of Fiji is a nation in the South Pacific Ocean comprised of three hundred thirty-two islands, of which about one hundred ten are permanently inhabited. The largest of these islands, Viti Levu, is about the same size as Jamaica.

The story of these fair and fertile islands, long the habitation of cruelty, is one of intense interest. That in 1845, an English plowboy who grew up without educational advantages should be, before his thirty-sixth year, the chief instrument in the conversion to Christianity and civilization of one of the most feral races of cannibals on earth is one of the most remarkable events in the history of Christian missions.

We cannot take time here to fully relate the wonderful story of John Hunt's missionary life. One scene will have to suffice to touch our hearts with the depth of this humble man's exploits in the power of the Spirit.

As the glorious reward of Mr. Hunt's labors and deep devotion, a great spiritual awakening finally took place. Among the converts was the Queen of Viwa.

"Her heart," said Mr. Hunt, "seemed literally to be broken, and, though a very strong woman, she fainted twice under the weight of a wounded spirit. She revived only to renew her strong cries and tears, so that it was all that we could do to proceed with the service.

"The effect soon became more general. Several of the women, and some of the men, literally roared for the disquietude of their hearts....It was very affecting to see upward of a hundred Fijians, many of whom were a few years ago some of the worst cannibals in the group, and even in the world, chanting, 'We praise Thee, O God; we acknowledge Thee to be the Lord,' while their voices were almost drowned by the cries of brokenhearted penitents."

Mr. Hunt's continuous toil at length took a serious toll on his health. The man of iron strength, who had come up to London from the fields of Lincolnshire only twelve years before, was evidently dying. Of him, as it was with his Lord, might it have been truly said, *"For the zeal of thine house hath eaten me up"* (Psalm 69:9).

With sad faces, the converts from heathenism flocked to the chapel and prayed earnestly for the missionary. "O Lord," Elijah Varani, the Fijian chief, cried aloud, "we know we are very bad, but spare Thy servant! If one must die, take me! Take ten of us! But spare Thy servant to preach Christ to the people!"

As Hunt neared the end, the missionary confidently committed his wife and babes to God but was sorely distressed for Fiji. Sobbing as though in acute distress, he cried, "Lord, bless Fiji! Save Fiji! Thou knowest my soul has loved Fiji—my heart has travailed for Fiji!"

Then, grasping his friend Calvert by the hand, he exclaimed again, "Oh, let me pray once more for Fiji! Lord, for Christ's sake, bless Fiji! Save Fiji!"

Turning to his mourning wife, he said, "If this be dying, praise the Lord!"

As his eyes looked up with a bright joy that defied death, he exclaimed, "I want strength to praise Him abundantly!" Then, with the cry of a triumphant "Hallelujah!" on his lips, he joined the worship of the skies.

—Adapted from William Fraser McDowell, *The Picket Line of Missions* (1897)

# Isabella Campbell (1827)

Oh, that I could tell you of the exceeding joy I have in the Lord Jesus Christ! How much is implied in those words, *'The peace of God, which passeth all understanding.'* I wish those who seek satisfaction in the things of time could understand a little of it.

"Live alone to God. Farewell!"

—Gottschall, *Selections from Testimonies and Dying Words*

# "Oh! Papa, What a Sweet Sight!"

*Submitted by Dr. L. B. Balliett of Allentown, Pennsylvania*

When ten-year-old Lillian Lee lay dying, she spoke to her father thus: "Oh! Papa, what a sweet sight! The golden gates are open, and crowds of children come pouring out. Oh, such crowds!"

Later, she cried, "They ran up to me and began to kiss me and call me by a new name. I can't remember what it was."

She then lay looking upward, her eyes dreaming. Her voice died to a whisper as she said, "Yes, yes, I come, I come!"

—Shaw, *Dying Testimonies of Saved and Unsaved*

# David Hume (1776)

David Hume, the deist philosopher and historian, was born in Edinburgh, Scotland, in 1711. In 1762, he published his work *Natural Religion*. Much of his time was spent in France, where he found many kindred spirits as vile and depraved as he.

He died in Edinburgh in 1776 at the age of sixty-five.

In his book *Modern Infidelity Considered* (1836), Rev. Robert Hall wrote,

> Infidelity is the joint offspring of an irreligious temper and unholy speculation, employed, not in examining the evidences of Christianity,

> but in detecting the vices and imperfections of confessing Christians. It has passed through various stages, each distinguished by higher gradations of impiety, for when men arrogantly abandon their guide, and willfully shut their eyes on the light of heaven, it is wisely ordained that their errors shall multiply at every step, until...the mischief of their principles works its own antidote.
>
> Hume was the most subtle, if not the most philosophical, of the deists. By perplexing the relations of cause and effect, he boldly aimed to introduce a universal skepticism and to pour a more than Egyptian darkness into the whole region of morals.

Again, in Bishop McIlvaine's *The Evidences of Christianity* (1877), we read,

> The nature and majesty of God are denied by Hume's argument against the miracles. It is atheism. There is no stopping place for consistency between the first principle of the essay of Hume and the last step in the denial of God. Hume, accordingly, had no belief in the existence of God. He did not positively deny it, yet he could not assert that he believed it. He was a poor, blind, groping compound of contradictions. He was literally "without God and without hope," "doting about questions and strifes of words," and rejecting life and immortality out of deference to a paltry quibble, of which common sense is ashamed.
>
> There is reason to believe that however unconcerned Hume may have seemed in the presence of his infidel friends, when not diverted by companions or cards, or his works and books of amusements, when left to himself and the contemplation of eternity, he was anything but composed and satisfied.
>
> The following account was published in Edinburgh, where he died. It is not known to have been ever contradicted. About the end of 1776, a few months after the historian's death, a respectable-looking woman, dressed in black, came into the Haddington stagecoach while passing through Edinburgh. The conversation among the passengers, which had been interrupted for a few minutes, was resumed, and the new passenger found it to be regarding the state of mind of persons at the prospect of death. In defense of infidelity, an appeal was made to the death of Hume as not only happy and tranquil, but mingled even with gaiety and humor.

To this, the lady said, "Sir, you know nothing about it; I could tell you another tale."

"Madam," replied the gentleman, "I presume I have as good information as you have on this subject, and I believe what I have asserted regarding Mr. Hume has never been called in question."

The lady continued, "Sir, I was Mr. Hume's housekeeper for many years and was with him in his last moments. The mourning I now wear is a present from his relatives for my attention to him on his deathbed. Happy would I have been if I could have borne my testimony to the mistaken opinion that has gone abroad of his peaceful and composed end. I have never till this hour opened my mouth on this subject, but I think it a pity the world should be kept in the dark.

"It is true, sir, that when Mr. Hume's friends were with him, he was cheerful and seemed quite unconcerned about his approaching fate. He even frequently spoke of it to them in a jocular and playful way. But when he was alone, the scene was very different—he was anything but composed. His mental agitation was so great at times as to occasion his whole bed to shake! And he would not allow the candles to be put out during the night, nor would he be left alone for a minute. I had always to ring the bell for one of the servants to be in the room before he would allow me to leave it.

"He struggled hard to appear composed, even before me. But to one who attended his bedside for so many days and nights and witnessed his disturbed sleep and still more disturbed waking—who frequently heard his involuntary breathings of remorse and frightful startings—it was no difficult matter to determine that all was not right within.

"This continued and increased until he became insensible. I hope to God I shall never witness a similar scene."

# Michelangelo Buonarroti (1564)

In a brief will, the great Italian painter and sculptor said, "I commit my soul to God, my body to the earth, my possessions to my nearest relatives. I die in the faith of Jesus Christ and in the firm hope of a better life."

His last words were, "Throughout life remember the sufferings of Jesus."

—Gottschall, *Selections from Testimonies and Dying Words*

# Bishop Joseph Butler (1752)

Upon his deathbed, Bishop Joseph Butler sent for his chaplain and said, "Though I have endeavored to avoid sin and please God, yet because of the consciousness of inner failure I am still afraid to die."

"My lord," answered the chaplain, "have you forgotten that Jesus Christ is a Savior?"

"True," continued the bishop, "but how shall I know that He is a Savior for me?"

"It is written, '*Him that cometh to me I will in no wise cast out*'" (John 6:37).

"True!" exclaimed the dying man. Then, he said, "I am surprised that, though I have read that Scripture a thousand times over, I never felt its virtue till this moment. Now I die happy."

—Johnstone, *Scottish Christian Herald*

# Walter C. Palmer (1883)

Dr. Palmer's biographer, Rev. George Hughes, wrote the following account:

At 5:15 p.m., July 20, 1883, Dr. Palmer's ransomed spirit entered the triumphal chariot and, under a bright angelic escort, sped away to the world of light and blessedness. There was no dark river to cross, no stormy billows to intercept his progress. It was a translation from the terrestrial to the celestial, the work of a moment but covered with eternal resplendency.

Heaven's pearly gates were surely opened wide to admit this battle-scarred veteran, laden with the spoils and honors of a thousand battles. The light of a conqueror was in his eye. His countenance was radiant. His language was triumphant. The angelic escort was near. The expanded vision was rapturously fixed on immortal objects and scenes. The ear was saluted with the songs of angels and redeemed spirits. The blood-washed soul was filled with high expectancy. Every avenue of the inner being was swept with rapture. Hallelujahs burst momentarily from his lips.

The aspect of such a departure was gorgeous indeed; no other word will express it. The splendors of the eternal state were gathered into a focus and burned intensely around the couch of the Christian warrior as he breathed his earthly farewell. He died only a few steps from his cottage-home, while the grand old ocean ceaselessly rolled its billows upon the sand, making solemn music and offering a deep-toned anthem of praise to the Creator. The clear, blue heavens above were resplendent. The sun was declining, but glorious in its decline.

Not far away was the hallowed grove, the place of holy song and gospel preaching, where multitudes congregated. And there, too, the "James Tabernacle," where such indescribable triumphs had been won. Even now, we seem to hear the forest resounding with prayer and praise.

Oh, the glorious scenes which those trees had witnessed:

In yonder cottage there is one newly born into the kingdom of heaven. The first song of the new life is breaking upon the ears of surrounding friends. Hallelujahs rule the hour.

In a little tent, there is a child of God who has just entered "Beulah Land"! He is inhaling its pure atmosphere. The fragrance of the land delights him. He is basking in the meridian rays of the "Sun of righteousness." What a heavenly glow there is upon his countenance! How the Beulah-notes burst from his lips!

Hark! Yonder is the shout of victory! What does it mean? Ah, one of God's dear saints has been sorely buffeted of Satan, but, "strong in the strength which God supplies through His eternal Son," she has just said, authoritatively, in overcoming faith, "Get thee behind me, Satan!" And, lo, the enemy is discomfited—he flies ingloriously from the field! Jesus, in the person of His tempted one, has driven the arch-foe to his native hell.

And so, we might go on and on. At each step, new wonders rise upon our view. Heaven and earth were surely keeping jubilee in this sacred enclosure.

Can we conceive of a grander spot, in either hemisphere, from which a good man might make his transition from world to world? Is it not written, *"My times are in thy hand"* (Psalm 31:15)? And are not the places, too, at the divine disposal? Did not Jehovah conduct His servant of old to the mount of transition and Himself perform the funeral rites and interment? And so secure was the entombment, so hidden from the rude gaze of men, that the ages have not discovered the burial place.

Is it too much to think that the God of glory put forth His hand to designate the place for the departure of His honored servant Dr. Palmer? And then, what a quiet hour—just as the sun was declining and the soft evening shades were being stretched forth! What an evening, after such a day!

All day long, the beloved one had been quietly reclining upon his couch. A new light had been given to his languid eye. A radiant smile illuminated his whole countenance. Inspiring words dropped from his lips. Loving friends, who had kept sleepless vigils around him, rejoiced with great joy.

The day had been a festive one. The table of the Lord had been spread before him, and he had feasted upon its dainties. At the foot of his couch had been suspended the book *The Silent Comforter*, telling of the riches of the kingdom of heaven. It was open at the passage for the day, reading thus:

*But now thus saith the LORD that created thee, O Jacob, and he that formed thee, O Israel, Fear not: for I have redeemed thee, I have called thee by thy name; thou art mine. When thou passest through the waters, I will be with thee; and through the rivers, they shall not overflow thee: when thou walkest through the fire, thou shalt not be burned; neither shall the flame kindle upon thee. For I am the LORD thy God, the Holy One of Israel, thy Saviour.*

(Isaiah 43:1–3)

What beautiful words—beautiful words of life! Well might that prostrate one rise into new life as he gazed upon the glittering pages. Indeed, he had, during the weeks of his suffering, taken refuge in the precious Word, so that the wicked one had not dared to approach him!

About two weeks before, Mrs. Palmer had said to him, "My dear, Satan has not troubled you much of late." Raising his arm, and with an emphatic voice, he exclaimed, "No! He has not been allowed to come near me!"

So strong was the doctor's returning pulse that those with him were encouraged to have him dressed and seated in an easy chair where he could look upon the ocean and be invigorated by its breezes. Indeed, he walked out and took his seat on the upper piazza. The beloved of his life was by his side, and a letter written later to a friend beautifully describes what transpired at this particular juncture:

"About three in the afternoon, he walked out on the second-story balcony, sat there a half hour or more, and seemed unusually joyous. He talked of the beautiful landscape before him and the grand old ocean. Seeing our dear friend Mr. Thornly, who had so kindly relieved us of the care of the morning meetings, our loved one waved his hand again and again, with smiles of affectionate recognition. He then went into the room and wrote a business letter to his son-in-law, Joseph F. Knapp, and read it to me in a strong voice.

"About five o'clock, he proposed lying down to rest. His head had scarcely reached the pillow when I was startled by seeing those large blue eyes open wide, as if piercing the heavens. Two or three struggles, as if for breath, followed.

"'Raise me higher,' he said, as I put my arm about him, holding him up. A moment's calm ensued. I said, 'Precious darling, it's passing over.' The dear one, putting his finger on his own pulse, looking so sweetly, said in a low tone, 'Not yet'—and almost in the same breath, in a clear, strong voice, he said, 'I fear no evil, for Thou art with me.'

"After a moment's pause, he continued, 'I have redeemed thee; thou art mine. When thou pass…' Here, his loved voice failed. The precious spirit was released to join the glorified above."

—Shaw, *Dying Testimonies of Saved and Unsaved*

Calconis was a pagan. However, while watching the martyrdom of two Christian brothers, their wonderful patience under terrible sufferings so struck him with admiration that he cried out, "Great is the God of the Christians!"

He himself was then immediately put to death.

—Gottschall, *Selections from Testimonies and Dying Words*

# "I Have Missed It at Last!"

Some time ago, a physician called on a young man who was ill. He sat by the bedside for a little while, examining his patient. Then, the doctor honestly told his patient that he had but a short time to live. The young man was astonished. He had forgotten that death often comes *"in such an hour as ye think not"* (Matthew 24:44).

At length, he looked up at the doctor and, with a most despairing countenance, said, "I have missed it at last!"

"What have you missed?" inquired the sympathizing physician.

"I have missed it at last," again he repeated.

"Missed what?"

"Doctor, I have missed the salvation of my soul."

"Oh, say not so—it is not so. Do you remember the thief on the cross?"

"Yes, I remember the thief on the cross. And I remember that he never said to the Holy Spirit, 'Go Your way!' But I did. And now, He is saying to me, 'Go your way!'"

The young man lay gasping awhile. Then, with a vacant, staring eye, he said, "I was awakened and was anxious about my soul a little time ago. But I did not want to be saved then. Something seemed to say to me, 'Don't put it off. Make sure of salvation.' I said to myself, *I will postpone it.* I knew I ought not to do it. I knew I was a great sinner and needed a Savior. I resolved, however, to dismiss the subject for the present. Yet, I could not get my own consent to do so until I had promised myself to take it up again, at a time more favorable. I bargained away, resisted, and insulted the Holy Spirit. I never thought of coming to this. I meant to have made my salvation assured, but now I have missed it!"

"Do you remember the parable in Matthew 20 of the laborers in the vineyard?" asked the doctor. "Do you remember that there were some who came to work in the vineyard at the eleventh hour, and everyone received the same reward?"

"My eleventh hour," he rejoined, "was when I had that call of the Spirit. I have had none since. I am given over to be lost. Oh, I have missed it! I have sold my soul for nothing—a feather, a straw. Now I am undone forever!"

This was said with such indescribable despondency that the doctor said nothing in reply. After lying a few moments, the young man raised his head and looked all around the room, as if searching for some desired object. Then he buried his face in the pillow and again exclaimed in agony and horror, "Oh, I have missed it at last!" Then he died.

Now is the accepted time!

*To day if ye will hear his voice, harden not your hearts.* (Hebrews 3:7–8)

—Shaw, *Dying Testimonies of Saved and Unsaved*

# Anne Camm
# (1705)

*A minister of the gospel in the Society of Friends*

I am the Lord's! His unspeakable peace I now enjoy. I am full of assurance of eternal salvation. The cross is the only way to the crown immortal. I have only one death to encounter."

—Gottschall, *Selections from Testimonies and Dying Words*

# Augustus M. Toplady
# (1778)

Augustus M. Toplady died in London on August 11, 1778, at the age of thirty-eight. He was the author of these immortal words:

Rock of Ages, cleft for me,
Let me hide myself in Thee;
Let the water and the blood,
From Thy wounded side which flowed,
Be of sin the double cure,
Save from wrath and make me pure.

Toplady had everything before him to make life desirable, yet when death drew near, his soul exulted in gladness. He said, "It is my dying avowal that these great and glorious truths, which the Lord, rich in mercy, has given me to believe and enabled me to preach, are now brought into practical and heartfelt experience. They are the very joy and support of my soul. The consolations flowing from them carry me far above the things of time and sense."

Frequently, Toplady called himself a dying man and yet the happiest man in the world, adding, "Sickness is no affliction, pain no curse, death itself no dissolution; and yet, how this soul of mine longs to be gone—like a bird imprisoned in its cage, it longs to take its flight. Had I wings like a dove, then would I fly away to the bosom of God and be at rest forever."

About an hour before he died, he seemed to awaken from slumber. "Oh, what delights! Who can fathom the joys of the third heaven? What a bright sunshine has been spread around me! I have not words to express it. I know it cannot be long now till my Savior will come for me, for...." He burst into a flood of tears as he continued, "Surely after the glories that God has manifested to my soul! All is light, light, light—the brightness of His own glory! O come, Lord Jesus, come—come quickly!"

Then he closed his eyes, his spirit going to be with Christ, his body falling asleep, to be awakened with others of like precious faith on that great day when the Lord Jesus shall be revealed from heaven with His mighty angels, *"to be glorified in his saints, and to be admired in all them that believe"* (2 Thessalonians 1:10).

—Davies, *Contrast Between Infidelity and Christianity*

# Clement Brown

When he was about to die, Clement Brown pointed with his finger and said, "I see one, two, three, four, five angels waiting their commission. I see them as plainly as I see you, Hester. How I wish you could see them! They are splendidly robed in white. They beckon me, and Jesus bids me come."

—Gottschall, *Selections from Testimonies and Dying Words*

# To Heaven and Back

*Submitted by Mrs. F. W. Strine of Dallas, Texas*

An older woman of our acquaintance told us a story that has greatly impressed me. She told of a time in her youth when she became very ill and was in the hospital for nine months with goiter and gland trouble. Her young husband watched over her with loving care, anxious that she should get well and be able to raise their two-year-old child.

One day, however, she felt her spirit leaving her body, and, looking back at the hospital room, she saw her husband weeping uncontrollably and the doctor shaking his head as they looked at her body lying on the bed.

When she got to heaven, she met an angel who, I suppose, was going to lead her on her way. Then she saw a young man and said, "Why, Tom, I didn't know you were up here."

He answered, "I didn't know you were here, either."

"I have just come," she said.

"So have I," he replied.

Suddenly, the angel said to the woman, "But you are going back to earth for a while."

For a moment, she was disappointed, for she thought that heaven was the most beautiful, peaceful, wondrous place—far beyond anything she had ever dreamed. Then, she thought of her husband and small child and said, "All right, I guess I should go back to them."

Suddenly, she was back on the bed in the hospital room. The doctor opened one of her eyes and exclaimed, "Why, this girl is going to live!" The doctor was so excited that he kissed her cheek.

Later, her husband was summoned to take a long-distance call. It was Tom's father. He said, "I have bad news for you. My son, Tom, has just been killed in an automobile accident."

# Return from Tomorrow

*Is it possible to have a glimpse into the next life? Dr. George C. Ritchie Jr.—a Richmond, Virginia, physician—answers this question with a step-by-step account of his amazing "Return from Tomorrow"*

When I was sent to the base hospital at Camp Barkeley, Texas, early in December 1943, I had no idea that I was seriously ill. I'd just completed army basic training, and my only thought was to board the train to Richmond, Virginia, and enter medical school as part of the army's doctor training program. It was an unusual break for a private, and I wasn't going to let a chest cold cheat me out of it.

But days passed. and I didn't get better. It was December 19 before I was moved to the recuperation wing, where a Jeep was to pick me up at four o'clock the next morning to drive me to the railroad station.

A few more hours and I'd make it! But around nine o'clock that evening, I began to run a fever. Despite my having taken some aspirin, my head continued to throb, and I coughed into the pillow to smother the sound. By three o'clock, I decided to get up and get dressed.

The next half hour is a blur to me. I remember being too weak to finish dressing. I remember a nurse coming to the room, and then a doctor, and then a bell-clanging ambulance ride to the X-ray building. I struggled unsteadily to my feet. I was able to stand long enough for them to take one image. The whir of the X-ray machine is the last thing I remember.

When I opened my eyes, I was lying in a room I had never seen before. A tiny light burned in a nearby lamp. For a while, I lay there, trying to recall where I was. All of a sudden, I sat bolt upright. The train! I would miss the train!

Now, I know that what I am about to describe will sound incredible. I do not understand it any more than I ask you to; all I can do is relate the events of that night as they occurred. I sprang out of bed and looked around the room for my uniform. It wasn't on the bedrail. I stopped, staring. Someone was lying in the bed I had just left.

I took a step closer in the dim light, then drew back. He was dead. The slack jaw and the gray skin were awful. Then, I saw the ring. On his left hand was the Phi Gamma Delta fraternity ring I had worn for two years.

I ran into the hall, eager to escape the mystery of that room. Richmond—that was the all-important thing. I had to get to Richmond. I started down the hall looking for the front door.

"Look out!" I shouted to an orderly bearing down on me. He seemed not to hear me, and a second later, he passed through the very spot in which I was standing, as though I was not even there.

It was too strange to think about. I reached the door and found myself in the darkness outside, speeding toward Richmond. Running? Flying? I know only that the dark earth was slipping past while other thoughts occupied my mind, terrifying and unaccountable ones. The orderly had not seen me. What if the people at medical school could not see me, either?

In utter confusion, I stopped by a telephone pole in a town by a large river and put my hand against the guy wire. At least the wire seemed to be there, but my hand could not make contact with it. One thing was clear: in some unimaginable way, I had lost my firmness of flesh—the hand that could grip the wire, the body that other people saw.

I also was beginning to realize that the body on that bed was mine, unaccountably separated from me, and that my job was to get back and rejoin it as fast as I could.

Finding the army base and hospital again was no problem. Indeed, I seemed to be back there almost as soon as I thought of it. But where was the little room I had left? So began what must have been one of the strangest searches ever to take place: the search for myself. As I ran from one ward to the next, past room after room of sleeping soldiers, all about my age, I realized how unfamiliar we are with our own faces. Several times, I stopped by a sleeping figure that was exactly as I imagined myself. But the fraternity ring was missing, and so I would speed on.

At last, I entered a little room with a single dim light. A sheet had been drawn over the figure on the bed, but the arms lay along the blanket. On the left hand was the ring.

I tried to draw back the sheet, but I could not seize it in my hand. And, now that I had found myself, how could one merge two people together who were so completely separate? There, standing before this problem, I thought, *This is death. This is what we human beings call "death," this splitting up of one's self.* It was the first time I had connected death with what had happened to me.

In that most despairing moment, the little room began to fill with light. I say "light," but there is no word in our language to describe brilliance that intense. I must try to find words, however, because, incomprehensible as the experience was to my intellect, it has affected every moment of my life since then.

The light that entered the room was Christ. I know this because a thought was put deep within me: *You are in the presence of the Son of God.*

I have called Him "light," but I could have also said "love," for that room was flooded, pierced, illuminated by the most total compassion I have ever felt. It was a Presence so comforting, so joyous and all-satisfying, that I wanted to lose myself forever in the wonder of it.

But something else was present in that room. With the presence of Christ—simultaneously, though I must tell it one by one—also had entered every single episode of my entire life. There they were—every event, thought, and conversation—as palpable as a series of pictures. There was no first or last; each one was contemporary; each one answered a single question: What did you do with your time on earth?

I looked anxiously among the scenes before me—school, home, scouting, the cross-country track team—a fairly typical boyhood, yet, in the light of that Presence, it seemed a trivial and irrelevant existence.

I searched my mind for good deeds.

*Did you tell anyone about Me?* came the question.

"I didn't have time to do much," I answered. "I was planning to, and then this happened. I'm too young to die!"

The thought was inexpressibly gentle: *No one is too young to die.*

A new wave of light spread through the room already so incredibly bright, and suddenly we were in another world. Or, rather, I suddenly perceived a different world occupying the same space all around me. I followed Christ through ordinary streets and countrysides, and everywhere I saw this other existence strangely superimposed on our familiar world.

It was thronged with people with the unhappiest faces I ever had seen. Each grief seemed different. I saw businessmen walking the corridors of the places where they had been working, trying vainly to get someone to listen to them. I saw a mother following a sixty-year-old man, her son, I guessed, cautioning him, instructing him. He did not seem to be listening.

Suddenly, I was remembering myself, that very night, caring about nothing but getting to Richmond. Was it the same for these people? Had their hearts and minds been concerned with earthly things, and now, having lost earth, were they still fixed hopelessly here? I wondered if this was hell. To care most when you are most powerless, that would be hell indeed.

I was permitted to look at two more worlds that night. I would not call them "spirit worlds," for they were too real, too solid. Both were introduced the same way: a new quality of light, a new openness of vision, and suddenly, it was apparent what had been there all along. The second world, like the first, occupied this very surface of the earth, but it was a vastly different realm.

Here there was no absorption with earthly things, but—for want of a better word to sum it up—only with truth.

I saw sculptors and philosophers, composers and inventors. There were universities and great libraries and scientific laboratories that surpass the wildest inventions of science fiction.

Of the final world, I had only a glimpse. Now we no longer seemed to be on earth but immensely far away and out of all relation to it. And there, still at a great distance, I saw a city—but a city, if such a thing is conceivable, constructed entirely out of light. At that time, I had not read the book of Revelation, or, incidentally, anything on the subject of life after death. But here was a city in which the walls, houses, and streets seemed to give off light, while moving among them were beings as blindingly bright as the One who stood beside me. This was only a momentary vision, for in the next instant, the walls of the little room closed around me, the dazzling light faded, and a strange sleep stole over me.

To this day, I cannot fathom why I was chosen to return to life. All I know is that when I woke up in the hospital bed of that little room, back in the familiar world where I had spent all my life, it was not a homecoming. The cry of my heart that moment has been the cry of my life ever since: *Christ, show me Yourself again!*

It was weeks before I was well enough to leave the hospital, and all that time, one thought obsessed me: *I need to look at my medical chart.* At last, the room was left unattended. There it was in terse medical shorthand: Pvt. George Ritchie, died December 20, 1943, double lobar pneumonia.

Later, I talked to the doctor who had signed the report. He told me that there was no doubt in his mind that I had been dead when he examined me, but that, nine minutes later, the soldier who had been assigned to prepare me for the morgue had come running to him to ask him to give me a shot of Adrenalin. The doctor gave me a hypo of Adrenalin directly into the heart muscle, all the while disbelieving what his own eyes were seeing. My return to life, he told me, without brain damage or other lasting effect, was the most baffling circumstance of his career.

Now, several decades later, I feel that I know why I had the chance to return to this life. It was to become a physician so that I could learn about man and then serve God. And every time I have been able to serve our God by helping some brokenhearted adult, treating some injured child, or counseling some teenager, deep within me, I have felt that He was there beside me, once again.

**Compiler's Note:** For decades, Dr. Ritchie spoke about his vision. He was active in youth work in Richmond, Virginia, and, in 1957, he founded the Christian Youth Corps of America with the purpose of developing character in young people. He also wrote a book about his life-after-death experience, *Return from Tomorrow.* Dr. George C. Ritchie finally returned to the source of his heavenly vision when he passed away on October 29, 2007.

# Elizabeth Barrett Browning (1861)

This famous English poetess declared, "We want the touch of Christ's hand upon our literature." Her last words were, "It is beautiful!"

—Gottschall, *Selections from Testimonies and Dying Words*

# The Dying Experience of a Wealthy Man

*How shall we escape, if we neglect so great salvation…?* (Hebrews 2:3–4)

A man, who shall remain anonymous, spent his life amassing a fortune without giving any attention to his soul's salvation. When he came to die, his wealth was no satisfaction to him. In fact, great anguish came on him as he fully realized that he had spent his life amassing wealth to the neglect of his soul.

In his dying condition, he called in his brother-in-law to pray for him. The brother-in-law said that the man called so loudly for mercy that he could scarcely hear himself pray or fix his thoughts on anything else. After the prayer was over, the dying man took his friend's hand in both of his and said, as he shook it, said, "Good-bye, John. Pray for me. I shall never see your face again." And he never did.

After the brother-in-law left, a neighbor came to visit, and, seeing the condition the man was in, he recommended that something be done. "I would suggest that we do something to quiet his mind and fears," he said. He offered to play a game of cards.

"Cards!" the dying man exclaimed. "Cards for a dying man! How contemptible. I'm going into eternity! These are not what I want. I want mercy!"

Later, that dying man's son came into his room and said, "Father, what arrangements, if any, do you wish to make in regard to the property?"

The dying man answered, "I have given all my life to gain property; I cannot take a dollar with me. The law and the family will have to take care of that. I want to take care of my soul. Property avails nothing. I want mercy!"

And so he died, calling on God for mercy, though he left no evidence that he found it.

—Shaw, *Dying Testimonies of Saved and Unsaved*

# Dying Without God

A youth at one of the large ironworks in Sheffield, England, was accidentally thrown onto a red-hot armor plate. When he was rolled off by his fellow workmen, nearly all of one side of his body was burned to the bone.

Some of the men cried, "Send for the doctor!" But the suffering youth cried, "Never mind the doctor! Is there anyone here who can tell me how to get saved? My soul has been neglected, and I'm dying without God. Who can help me?"

There were three hundred men around him, but not one could tell him the way of salvation. After twenty minutes of untold agony, he died as he had lived—without God.

Among those who witnessed this accident and heard the cries of the dying youth was a Christian who had fallen back into a sinful life. When I asked him about the incident, he said, "I have heard his cries ever since and so wished I could have stooped down and pointed him to Jesus, but my life closed my lips."

Does our life tell the world that we are Christians, or does it close our lips when others need us most?

—Shaw, *Dying Testimonies of Saved and Unsaved*

# Sir David Brewster (1835)

This distinguished Scottish scientist in the field of optics died saying, "I shall see Jesus, and that will be grand. I shall see Him who made the worlds."

—Gottschall, *Selections from Testimonies and Dying Words*

# A Young Man Returns to Tell of Heaven

*The following remarkable testimony was told by George B. Hilty to his daughter, Mrs. Carol Reeves, of Hammett, Idaho. I knew the Hiltys for many years and even faintly remember David Hilty. Through the years, I've heard this testimony several times. In essence, the retelling has proved consistent.*

*—Paul W. Miller, Hammett, Idaho*

In 1893, the Lord was speaking to David Hilty, a middle-aged, uneducated Mennonite farmer in Hancock County, Ohio. God was calling him to yield himself to the service of ministering to his brethren, but David could not see how a holy God could use such a man as he. Thus, he would not surrender to the call.

During this time, David bought a different farm and moved into a house where, unknown to him, the former owners had died of tuberculosis. Over time, one member of the Hilty family after another became ill with this terrible disease. Two had bones in their legs infected, and the oldest son, Will, developed a lung infection.

One day, they realized that Will—nearly twenty-one years old—was dying. His life was slipping away from his body, but his spirit was in such communion with his Lord that he told them he would be going home in two weeks.

Then, one morning, little Elizabeth—the baby of the family, just five years old—told several members of the family that she was going to heaven, too. "Jesus is going to take me home right away," she said. It was as if she was happy to have received an invitation to be the first to go on the journey her brother Will spoke of so often.

The parents had planned a trip to Michigan by wagon, but they decided to postpone it for a few days until their little girl recovered from her unnatural ideas about death. That very day, however, Elizabeth was quiet and seemed unusually tired. Toward evening, she became feverish and ill. About four o'clock the next morning, she went to be with Jesus, who had told her that He would be taking her home "right away."

As the last days of Will's life passed, he continued to praise and glorify God the Father and Jesus His Son, pleading with all who visited to be converted and to believe. Through cracked and bleeding lips, he spoke of the surpassing joy of knowing Christ!

He longed to be released from his pain-filled body, and on the very day he had prophesied that he would go, he fell asleep in death.

But their mother's heart could not bear to say good-bye to another child. She refused to be consoled. Will's brother John also felt torn with grief, and, kneeling on the opposite side of the bed from his mother, he, too, wept and called, "Will, don't die yet!"

Moments passed, but the hearts of those who mourned Will's passing could find no calm. Suddenly, a sister standing at the foot of the bed exclaimed, "Look, didn't Will's eyelids flutter?" All watched breathlessly as the still form stirred and breath again came through the blistered lips.

"Mother, John, don't weep for me. Don't call me back. I've been with Jesus, and the glory and wonder of it is so great! Your grief hurt me, and I asked permission to come and tell you to be glad. I had to promise not to tell you the secrets that God has prepared for His saints, but I want you to know that it is far, far more wonderful than anything you can imagine!"

Will's face shone with a heavenly light as he comforted his parents, brothers, and sisters. When he again said, "Good-bye" and left, they were able to rejoice in his joy and believe that this was only a temporary separation.

David Hilty answered the call to become a pastor. He allowed the power of God to change him into a new man and an able teacher of the Word. The experience of this supernatural act and the presence of the Holy Spirit that was so evident in his resurrected son, Will, completely melted the unbelief that had held him bound.

# John Brooks (1825)

*Governor of Massachusetts*

I see nothing terrible in death. In looking to the future, I have no fears, for I know in whom I have believed. I look back on my past life with humility, and I am sensible of many imperfections that cleave to me, but I now rest my soul on the mercy of my Creator, through the only Mediator, His Son, our Lord Jesus.

"Oh, what a ground of hope there is in that saying of the apostle that God is in Christ, reconciling the guilty world to Himself, not imputing their trespasses unto them."

He put out his hand and was asked, "What are you reaching for?"

"A kingdom!" he whispered, just as he passed away.

—Gottschall, *Selections from Testimonies and Dying Words*

# Carrie Carmen's Vision of the Holy City

Young Carrie Carmen lay at death's door, perfectly conscious. Suddenly, she gazed upward and exclaimed, "Beautiful! Beautiful! Beautiful!"

Someone asked, "What is so beautiful?"

"Oh," she exclaimed, "they are so beautiful."

"What do you see?"

"Angels!" Carrie said. "And they are so beautiful."

"How do they look?"

"Oh, I can't tell you. They are so beautiful."

"Have they wings?"

"Yes. Listen! They sing the sweetest of anything I have ever heard."

"Do you see Christ?"

"No, but I see the Holy City that was measured with the reed, whose length and breadth and height are equal, and whose top reaches to the skies. It is so beautiful; I can't tell you how splendid it is."

Then, she quoted a hymn, saying, "Through the valley of the shadow I must go." She also spoke of the loneliness of her husband, praying that he might have grace to bear his bereavement and that strength might be given him to go out and labor for souls, for they were expecting soon to enter the ministry. She also prayed for her parents, asking that they might make an unbroken band in the beautiful city.

She closed her eyes and rested a moment, then looked up with beaming eyes and said, "I see Christ, and oh, He is so beautiful!"

Her husband asked, "How does He look?"

"I can't tell you, but He is so much more beautiful than all the rest." Again, she said, "I see the Holy City." Then, after gazing a moment longer, she said, "So many!"

"What do you see, of which there are so many?"

"People," she said.

"How many are there?"

"A great many—more than I can count."

"Any you know?"

"Yes, a great many."

"Who?"

"Uncle George, and a lot more. They are calling me; they are beckoning to me."

"Is there any river there?"

"No, I don't see any."

Her husband then said, "Carrie, do you want to go and leave me?"

"No, not until it is the Lord's will that I should go. I would like to stay and live for you and for God's work. His will be done."

Presently, she lifted her eyes and said, "Oh, carry me off from this bed."

Her husband said, "She wants to be removed from the bed."

But her father said, "She is talking with the angels."

When asked if this was so, she replied, "Yes."

She then thanked the doctor for his kindness and asked him to meet her in heaven. She closed her eyes and seemed to be sinking rapidly away.

Her husband tenderly kissed her and said, "Carrie, can't you kiss me?"

She opened her eyes again and kissed him, saying, "Yes, I can come back to kiss you. I was partway over."

She said little more but prayed for herself and for her friends. Frequently, she would gaze upward and smile as though the sights were very beautiful.

—Martin Wells Knapp, *Christ Crowned Within* (1886)

# James Guthrie
## (1661)

Just before being beheaded, this Scottish minister cried, "The covenants shall yet be Scotland's reviving. I would not exchange this scaffold for the palace!"

—Gottschall, *Selections from Testimonies and Dying Words*

# Caliph Abd-ar-Rahman III
## (961)

*Emir and Caliph of Córdoba, Spain*

I have now reigned above fifty years in victory or peace, beloved by my subjects, dreaded by my enemies, and respected by my allies. Riches and honors, power and pleasure, have waited on my call; nor does any earthly blessing appear to have been wanting to my felicity. In this situation, I have diligently numbered the days of pure and genuine happiness which have fallen to my lot: they amount to fourteen. O man! Place not thy confidence in this present world!"

—Gottschall, *Selections from Testimonies and Dying Words*

# Thomas Haukes (1555)

After being condemned to death at the stake, Thomas Haukes agreed with his friends that if God would give him grace to so endure the pains of burning as to show some sign, he would raise his hands above his head before dying.

With a strong chain about his waist, he addressed the crowd, and as the fire was kindled, he poured out his soul to God in prayer. Soon, his speech was taken away by the violence of the flames, his skin drawn together, and his fingers consumed. When everyone thought he was dead, suddenly, and contrary to all expectation, he reached up his burning hands and clapped them together three times. Then, sinking down in the fire, he gave up his spirit.

# "I Am in the Flames! Pull Me Out! Pull Me Out!"

*Adapted from an article by Rev. C. A. Balch of Cloverville, New York*

Mr. W—, the subject of this narrative, died in New York about the year 1883 at the age of seventy-four. He was an avowed infidel. He was a good neighbor in some respects, but he was very wicked and scoffed at Christianity. About seven years prior to his death, he attended a revival, and the Spirit strove with him, but he resisted to the last.

One Sunday after this, a local lay preacher who related this sketch, while on his way to church passed Mr. W—'s house and saw him standing by the gate. The preacher said, "Come with me to church, Mr. W—."

The infidel, holding out his hand, replied, "Show me a hair on the palm of my hand, and I will show you a Christian."

When Mr. W— was stricken with his last sickness, it was this preacher who called on him often, sat up with him several nights, and even was with him when he died. The infidel was conscious of his near-approaching end, and then, when it was too late, he also was conscious of the terrors of his lost condition.

On one occasion, he said, "Warn the world not to live as I have lived and to escape my woe."

At another time, when visited by a doctor, he was groaning and making demonstrations of great agony. The doctor asked, "Why do you groan? Your disease is not painful."

"Oh, doctor," Mr. W— said, "it is not the body but the soul that troubles me!"

On the evening of his death, as he entered the room with a friend, the preacher felt that it was filled with an awful presence—as if this sick man were near the region of the damned. The dying man cried out, "Oh God, deliver me from that awful pit!"

It was not a penitential prayer but the wail of a lost soul.

About fifteen minutes before his death, which happened to occur at midnight, he exclaimed, "I am in the flames! Pull me out, pull me out!" He kept repeating this, and as his strength failed, his words became more faint. At last, the preacher put his ear down close to catch his departing whispers. The last words he heard were these: "Pull me out! Pull me out!"

"It was an awful experience," the preacher said later. "It made an impression on me that I can never forget. I never want to witness such a scene again."

Years later, when I was talking to this preacher, he told me that those last terrible words, "I am in the flames! Pull me out, Pull me out!" were still ringing in his ears.

> *And cast ye the unprofitable servant into outer darkness: there shall be weeping and gnashing of teeth.* (Matthew 25:30)

> *Then shall he say also unto them on the left hand, Depart from me, ye cursed, into everlasting fire, prepared for the devil and his angels.... And these shall*

*go away into everlasting punishment: but the righteous into life eternal.*
(Matthew 25:41, 46)

—Shaw, *Dying Testimonies of Saved and Unsaved*

# God's Grace to a "Weak Believer"

*An experience from the compiler, John Myers*

In December 1966, my dear mother died of cancer. She could have been called a "weak believer." By this, I mean that her spiritual roots were not deep enough to enable her to face death with a sense of victory. It was obvious that she dreaded it and avoided every mention of the subject. This concerned us, and we prayed definitely.

As the end neared, she clung to life, fearing to take the plunge into the unknown. However, when finally she was forced over the edge of that cliff, she found that though she believed not, *"yet he abideth faithful"* (2 Timothy 2:13), and underneath were those everlasting arms. (See Deuteronomy 33:27.) She died with a definite testimony.

The day before the end, she said, "I asked the Lord to take me last night, but He said it wasn't time yet."

Having been called away on business several days earlier, I was hastening to Mom's bedside at this time. She had been very reluctant to see me go, and I had promised that I would return. It would have been a crushing blow if she had died before I arrived. Perhaps this is the reason the Lord told her it wasn't yet time. She remained conscious less than an hour after my arrival.

Then, when the doctor came in, she simply said to him, "I am ready to die."

When we asked if she had actually talked with the Lord, she answered, in effect, "Of course"—as if there was nothing at all unusual about this.

To me, this was a triumph of God's love and grace. If Mom had been a strong Christian and, with great faith, had marched boldly into the jaws of death, one might have *expected* the Lord to so respond; but when He did so anyway, despite her weakened faith, it revealed His great, tender heart of love. Truly, all the glory was His! Also, we thank Him and were so comforted that Mom's passing was not complicated by the great pain that usually accompanies cancer of this sort.

But the story doesn't end there, for the tidings of one victory often touch off others. The above account of my mother's passing was included in my ministry newsletter for the months of January/February 1967, and we later received the following note from a subscriber:

> Right after I received the newsletter in which Mr. Myers told about his mother's death, I went home to see my cousin, who also was dying from cancer. He had just accepted the Lord at the beginning of his illness, and he didn't want to die so young—only thirty-one. He kept telling his father this, and I could not help but remember the newsletter.
>
> I felt led to pray for him in the same way that Mr. Myers did for his dear mother. And from then on, he wasn't afraid to die. I could just feel the presence of the Lord and His great love wrapping my cousin up in that love. He was at peace from then on.
>
> Oh, it was such a blessing to know that I could ask the Lord to love him so much that he wouldn't be afraid. And it all came from remembering the newsletter. So, may your hearts be lifted up in praise, too, for I'm sure that many people have had a share in these blessings!

# Romanus of Caesarea
## (c. 303)

Romanus, a native of Palestine, was deacon of the church of Caesarea at the commencement of Emperor Diocletian's persecution in the fourth century. He was at Antioch when the imperial order came requiring the sacrifice of animals to idols, and he was grieved to see many Christians, through fear, submit to the command that they deny their faith in order to preserve their lives.

While reproving some of them for their weakness, Romanus was informed on and, soon after, arrested. At his tribunal, he confessed to being a Christian and expressed his willingness to suffer any punishment they would choose to inflict on him for his confession. When condemned, he was scourged and put to the rack, his body torn with hooks.

While thus cruelly mangled, he turned to the governor and thanked him for having opened for him so many mouths with which to preach Christianity. "For," he said, "every wound is a mouth to sing the praises of the Lord."

Soon after, he was slain by strangulation.

—Shaw, *Dying Testimonies of Saved and Unsaved*

# "You'll Be a Duke, but I Shall Be a King!"

Tuberculosis seized the eldest son and heir of the Duke of Hamilton and brought him to an early death. Just before his departure from the world, he lay ill at the family home near Glasgow, Scotland.

Two ministers came to see him. At his request, one of them prayed with him. After the minister had prayed, the dying youth reached back, produced a Bible from under his pillow, and opened it and read aloud,

> *I have fought a good fight, I have finished my course, I have kept the faith: henceforth there is laid up for me a crown of righteousness, which the Lord, the righteous judge, shall give me at that day: and not to me only, but unto all them also that love his appearing.* (2 Timothy 4:7–8)

"This, sirs," said he, "is all my comfort."

Later, as he was lying on the sofa, his tutor was conversing with him on some astronomical subject and about the nature of the fixed stars.

"Ah," said the young man, "in a little while, I shall know more of this than all of you together."

As his death approached, he called his brother to his bedside and, addressing him with the greatest affection and seriousness, closed with these remarkable words: "And now, Douglas, in a little time, you'll be a duke, but I shall be a king!"

—Shaw, *Dying Testimonies of Saved and Unsaved*

# An Atheist Said...

There is one thing that mars all the pleasure of my life. I am afraid the Bible is true. If I could only know for a certainty that death is an eternal sleep, I should be happy. But here is what pierces my soul: if the Bible is true, I am lost forever!"

*"The fool hath said in his heart, There is no God"* (Psalm 14:1).

—Shaw, *Dying Testimonies of Saved and Unsaved*

# Sir Philip Sidney (1586)

Sir Philip Sidney was born in 1554 in Kent, England. He possessed shining talents, was well-educated, and, at the early age of twenty-one, was sent by Queen Elizabeth as her ambassador to the emperor of Germany.

He is described by the writers of that age as the finest model of an accomplished gentleman that could be formed, even in imagination. An amiable disposition, elegant erudition, and polite conservation rendered him the ornament and delight of the English court. Lord Brooke so highly valued his friendship that he directed the following to be inserted as part of his epitaph: "Here lies Sir Philip Sidney's friend." Sidney's fame was so widely spread that if he had chosen it, he might have obtained the crown of Poland.

But the glory of this Marcellus of the English nation was of short duration. When he was only thirty-two years old, he was wounded at the Battle of Zutphen and died within about three weeks.

After being brought into a tent because of his fatal wound, Sidney raised his eyes toward heaven and acknowledged the hand of God in this event. He confessed himself a sinner and thanked God that "He had not struck him with death at once, but gave him space to seek repentance and reconciliation."

In the light of his new understanding of God, his former virtues seemed as nothing. When it was said to him that good men in the time of great affliction find comfort and support in the recollection of those parts of their lives in which they had glorified God, he humbly replied, "It is not so with me. I have no comfort that way. All things in my former life have been vain."

When asked whether he did not desire life, merely to have it in his power to glorify God, he answered, "I have vowed my life unto God, and if He cut me not off and suffer me to live longer, I shall glorify Him and give up myself to His service."

The nearer death approached, the more his consolation and hopes increased. A short time before the end, he lifted his eyes and hands and uttered these words: "I would not change my joy for the empire of the world!"

His advice and observations when saying farewell to his deeply afflicted brother are worthy of remembrance: "Love my memory; cherish my friends. Their fidelity to me may assure you that they are honest. But, above all, govern your wills and affections by the will and Word of your Creator. In me, behold the end of the world and all its vanities."

—Lindley Murray, *The Power of Religion on the Mind in Retirement, Sickness, and at Death; Exemplified in the Testimonies and Experience of Men Distinguished by Their Greatness, Learning, or Virtue* (1787)

# "Jesus Will Take Care of Me"

These were the last words uttered by twelve-year-old Ella Gilkey as she passed away from earth to live with Him who said, *"Suffer little children, and forbid them not, to come unto me: for of such is the kingdom of heaven"* (Matthew 19:14).

In the winter of 1860–1861, I was holding a series of meetings in Watertown, Massachusetts, during which a large number of people found Jesus precious—many believing they found Him in my room, thus rendering that room ever memorable and dear to me.

Among those there who gave themselves to the Savior was Ella. Coming in one morning with tears on her face, she said, "Mr. Earle, I came up here to give my heart to Jesus. I feel that I am a great sinner. Will you pray for me?"

I replied, "I will pray for you, Ella, and I can pray in faith if you see that you are a sinner—for Jesus died for sinners."

After pointing out the way of salvation, I asked if she would kneel down by my side, pray for herself, and give herself to Jesus, to be His forever.

She said, "I will, for I am a great sinner."

Could one so young and kind to everybody be a great sinner? Yes, because she had rejected the Savior until she was twelve years old. Whenever the Holy Spirit had knocked at the door of her heart, she had said, in effect, "No, not yet. Go Thy way for this time."

We kneeled down, and, after I had prayed, she said, "Jesus, take me just as I am. I give myself to Thee forever. I will love and serve Thee all my life."

The door of her heart was now open, and Jesus entered and took possession. When she arose, the tears were gone from her face, and it was covered with a beautiful smile. I believe that holy angels witnessed the transfer of her heart to Jesus and then went back to heaven to join in songs of thanksgiving, for the Bible says, *"Joy shall be in heaven over one sinner that repenteth"* (Luke 15:7).

Then, Ella went downstairs, her face beaming with joy as she thought of her new relationship to Jesus. She at once said to her mother, "I have given myself to Jesus, and He has received me. Oh, I am so happy!"

Little did we think that in only a few weeks, she would be walking the golden streets with the blood-washed throng. Like the Redeemer, who, when her age, said to His mother, *"How is it that ye sought me? wist ye not that I must be about my Father's business?"* (Luke 2:49), she seemed to long to be doing good.

"What can I do for Christ," she said, "who gave His life to ransom me? I'll take my cross and by Him be led; His humble, faithful child will be."

Among other subjects of prayer, there was one that particularly weighed upon her heart: for the conversion of an older brother. One day, after earnestly praying that this dear brother might be led to accept the Savior, she said to her mother, "Oh, I think he will be a Christian!" At another time, she said, "I would be willing to die if it would bring him to Jesus."

Anxious to obey her Savior in all things, she obtained permission from her parents to present herself for baptism, and, in the absence of a pastor, I baptized her along with several others a few weeks after her conversion.

The following Tuesday, she was present at our evening meeting and gave her last public testimony for Jesus. Facing the congregation, she said in a clear, earnest tone, "If there are any here who have not given their hearts to Jesus, do it now."

I was staying at the Gilkey home, and as I sat in my room that night after meeting, I heard Ella's sweet voice mingling with her father's in songs of praise until near the midnight hour.

Less than three days later, she was called away from us to sing with the angels in heaven the song of Moses and the Lamb.

As death drew near, she said to her parents, "I am going home," and she commenced singing her favorite hymn:

O happy day, that fixed my choice
On Thee, my Savior and my God!
Well may this glowing heart rejoice,
And tell its raptures all abroad.

"Yes," she whispered, "it *was* a happy day." Then, looking up at her father, whose heart seemed almost broken, she slipped her arm around his neck and said, "Don't care for me, Father. Jesus will take care of me."

These were her last conscious words. The smile of affection on her face, the look of love in her eyes, and its pressure in her hand, lingered a little longer, and then her spirit took its flight.

On the first Sunday of February, the church gave the hand of fellowship to a large number of new members. Ella would have been with them, had she lived. It so happened that near the place where she would have stood, there was a vacant spot. I directed the attention of the large assembly to that opening and asked, "Where is Ella today?"

For a moment, all was still, as the entire congregation appeared to be bathed in tears. Then, I said, "Jesus seems to say, 'I have given Ella the hand of fellowship up here.'"

A few days after her death, her parents were looking over her school things. In the middle of a blank book unknown to anyone, as if intended only for God's eye, they found the following statement, which shows her depth of purpose and complete dedication to Christ:

> December 21, 1860. This day I have given my heart to the Savior and have resolved to do just what He tells me to do and to take up my cross daily and follow Him—my eyes to weep over sinners, and my mouth to speak forth His praise and lead sinners to Christ.
>
> —Ella J. Gilkey

In the vestry of the church at Watertown, these words, printed in large type and beautifully framed, now hang on the wall, where all who enter may read them. So, in the hours of Sunday school, the prayer meetings, and social gatherings, little Ella, though in heaven, still speaks and continues her work for Jesus.

—Shaw, *Dying Testimonies of Saved and Unsaved*

# Adoniram Judson
# (1850)

This famous American missionary to Burma died at sea. His last words were, "I go with the gladness of a boy bounding away from school. I feel so strong in Christ."

—Gottschall, *Selections from Testimonies and Dying Words*

# "I Saw the Black Angel"

The following letter is from Mrs. Robert Snyder at Prairie Bible Institute in Three Hills, Alberta, Canada:

> Because of a sad misunderstanding—perhaps because of pride on my part—I allowed my fifteen-year-old daughter to be in Southern California for a whole summer without visiting her grandmother.
>
> This was such a terrible disappointment for my mother that she became ill. I was told that she was in the hospital for three weeks, hovering between life and death.
>
> Can you imagine how I felt? The Word of God is needed at such a time to divide between soul and spirit. He showed me how much my motives needed purifying. But thank God for a merciful and faithful High Priest, who is touched with the feeling of our infirmities. What do you think our loving and merciful God did? He visited Mama in that hospital room, raised her up, and gave her a new song and a testimony that never wavered!
>
> Then, three years later, when He took her home, He united our family as never before. But I'll let her tell it, in a letter from November 11, 1962:
>
>> Nita, I sure almost went over this time. I saw the black angel standing by my bed, but then, someone else with a sweet, smiling face came, and I went to sleep. When I awakened, I knew I'd get well, but it was the one with the lovely, sweet face who let me stay for a while longer. I wasn't one bit frightened. Indeed, I shut my eyes to say, "Thank You, Lord, for my release," then opened them, and this smiling one was there—a wonderful experience. So, now I must find out what I'm left over another time to do.
>
> Then, a remarkable thing happened: the Holy Spirit recalled to Mama's mind a song she used to sing in an old Texas Methodist camp meeting after her conversion. It was from a time more than sixty years

prior—think of the power of God's Spirit to recall memories! Mama later got up and sang this song before about one hundred people:

Night, with ebon pinions brooded o'er the vale;
All around was silence, save the night wind's wail,
When Christ, the Man of Sorrows,
In tears, and sweat, and blood,
Prostrate in the garden, raised His voice to God.

Smitten for offences which were not His own,
He, for our transgressions, had to weep alone;
No friend with words of comfort,
Nor hand to help was there,
When the Meek and Lowly humbly bowed in prayer.

"Abba, Father, Father, if it may,
Let this cup of anguish pass from Me, I pray;
Yet, if it must be suffered, by Me, Thine only Son,
Abba, Father, Father, let Thy will be done."[2]

# Ann Knight (1806)

"This has been a blessed night to me. I have seen heaven, and they are all happy, so happy there. The Almighty has been so near to me. I feel that He was asking me to let go of all the world—which I can freely do—to possess that peace and happiness I have seen."

—Gottschall, *Selections from Testimonies and Dying Words*

2. Love H. Jameson, "Night, with Ebon Pinion," 1854.

# The "Valley of the Shadow" Was Bridged Over

In her 1896 book, *Wayside Sketches*, Sarah A. Cooke, widely known in the nineteenth century for her writings and evangelistic work, gave an account of the last days of her sister, who died in England during the spring of 1864.

> I was called to the sickbed of my eldest sister, Eliza, living in Melton Mowbray, Leicestershire. I found her suffering from intermittent fever and general prostration.
>
> During the first stage of her sickness, there seemed a strong clinging to life. Very happy in her marriage, surrounded by a circle of loving friends, and being an earnest worker in the cause of the Redeemer, life for Eliza was full of attraction. Then also came the thought of her husband's loneliness without her, and she said, "I would be quite willing to go, but Harry would miss me so much."
>
> Finally, however, faith triumphed over nature, and she said, "The Lord could make Harry a happy home if He should take me."
>
> Day by day, the attraction heavenward became stronger. Once, when all was fixed for the night and I was leaving the room, she called to me. Looking earnestly into my face, she said, "Sarah, don't pray for my recovery." I reminded her how much we all loved her, but she answered, "And I love you all very much, but it is so much better to depart and be with Jesus."
>
> While with her during the day, listening to the doctor's cheery and hopeful words, I would think she might recover, but in prayer, I could never take hold for her health. I could only breathe out, "Thy will, O Lord, not mine, be done."
>
> The prayer of faith, in which at times our Father enables His children to take hold for the healing of the body, was never given. In His infinite

love and wisdom, He was calling her home, "where no storms ever beat on that beautiful strand, while the years of eternity roll."

Every afternoon, she liked to be left entirely alone for about an hour. The fever would then be off, and she chose it as the best time for secret communion with the Lord. When I opened the door one day, after the hour had passed, she sat upright in bed, her face simply radiant with joy as she exclaimed, "Oh, I have had such a view of God's love!"

Stretching out her hands, she said, "It seems to me like a boundless ocean—as though I were lost in that boundless ocean of love!"

When suffering from extreme prostration, her favorite lines would be:

> Christ leads us through no darker rooms
> Than He went through before;
> He that unto God's kingdom comes
> Must enter by this door.[3]

A dear friend said to her one day, "Do you have any fear of death?"

"Oh no," she answered, "I don't know that I have ever thought of it." The word "death" was never on her lips. The *"valley of the shadow"* (Psalm 23:4) was bridged over. She did not see it, for the eye of faith swept over it and was fixed upon Him who is the resurrection and the life. "To be with Jesus!" was her oft-repeated expression.

On Friday, with tenderest, deepest joy, she repeated another beautiful hymn:

> "Forever with the Lord!"
> Amen, so let it be!
> Life from His death is in that word,
> 'Tis immortality.
> Here in the body pent,
> Absent from Him I roam,
> Yet nightly pitch my moving tent
> A day's march nearer home.[4]

---

3. Richard Baxter, "Lord, It Belongs Not to My Care," 1681.
4. James Montgomery, "Forever with the Lord," 1835.

Sunday was her last day on earth. Seeing the end was very near, I hesitated about leaving to teach her Bible class, a large class of young women, at the chapel. I had been teaching them every Sunday afternoon.

"Would you like me, dear, to take your class this afternoon?" I asked softly.

"Yes," she answered, with some surprise in her voice, "why not?" It was a melting time as we together realized how near the parting was. Finally, she said, "Tell them all I have loved and prayed for them very much."

The lesson that day was the words of comfort our Savior had spoken to His disciples, as recorded in chapter 14 of the gospel of John. Afterward, I invited the whole class home, and they all passed by the open door to take a last look at their beloved teacher. Wonderfully, all through the day, the words that I had taught the girls were applied to my own heart, *"If ye loved me, ye would rejoice, because I said, I go unto the Father"* (John 14:28). The thought of her exceeding blessedness in being so near the presence of Jesus swallowed up all thoughts of sorrow at losing her.

Hour after hour passed, as the "silver cord" was loosening. An aunt who was present remarked, "You have had seven weeks of peace."

"I have had seven weeks of perfect peace," Eliza answered. Truly, her peace flowed like a river all through the day.

With her head leaning on the bosom of her husband, the last words our listening ears caught were, "Though I walk through the valley of the shadow of death, I will fear no evil, for Thou art with me."

# Judgment in a Young Man

The following incident from the pen of Sister M. A. Sparling, of Claremont, New Hampshire, is an illustration that *"the wicked is snared in the work of his own hands"* (Psalm 9:16). She wrote:

A few years ago, I was at a camp meeting in Rockingham, Vermont, when a gang of rowdies got together to break up our gathering. They lived eight miles away, but on Thursday evening, they came to the camp grounds to "have their fun," as they told some of their friends. The plan was to lay trails of powder into every tent and under the beds. When the town clock struck twelve midnight, all were to touch fire to the powder, then run to a distance and see the frightened women and children run and scream.

At ten o'clock, distant thunder was heard, and, before midnight, God sent one of the most terrific thunderstorms I have ever witnessed. It had been a warm day, and these young men had no coats with them. Now, with their powder all wet and their plans defeated, they were compelled to ride the eight miles back to their homes, drenched with rain and chilled through and through.

The ringleader had to be carried into his house, benumbed with cold. For hours, his mother tried to get him warm. Then came a burning fever. He told her what he had planned to do, saying, "Mother, I've got to die! Do pray! Do pray! What shall I do? Oh, how can I die?"

She said, "I never prayed."

"Then call Father," cried the dying man. But the father could not pray, either.

Then he cried, clutching his hands and wringing them in agony, "I can't die so! I can't die so! Mother, Mother, do pray! Do pray!"

The father went to a Baptist deacon, but before he arrived, the young man was past help. With distorted eyes, hands uplifted over his head and writhing in agony, he died raving. Among his last words were, "I'm going to hell! I'm lost, lost, lost! I can't die so! I can't, I can't! Oh, Mother, it's awful to go to hell this way!"

—Gottschall, *Selections from Testimonies and Dying Words*

# Basilides
# (235)

Basilides was the captain of a party of heathen persecutors who executed the female martyr Potamiena. He had shown her some kindness in shielding her from the mob, and to repay his kindness, the virgin girl said she would pray for him.

Soon afterward, he became a Christian and was beheaded. Before his execution, when asked the cause of his sudden decision to cast his lot with the saints, he said that Potamiena, three days after her martyrdom, stood by him in the night and put a crown upon his head. She said that she had entreated the Lord for him and that her request had been granted.

— Gottschall, *Selections from Testimonies and Dying Words*

# "Ma, I Can't Die till You Promise Me"

At the close of a series of meetings in Springfield, Massachusetts, a mother handed me a little girl's picture wrapped in two one-dollar bills, at the same time relating the following touching incident.

The picture was of her only child. At the age of six, she gave her heart to the Savior, giving, as the pastor with whom I was laboring said, the clearest evidence of conversion.

At once, she went to her mother and said, "Ma, I have given my heart to Jesus, and He has received me; now, won't you give your heart to Him?"

The mother replied, "I hope I shall sometime, dear Mary."

The little girl urged the mother, with all her childlike earnestness, to give herself to the Savior right then, saying, "Do it now, Ma!"

Finding that she could not prevail in that way, the girl sought to secure a promise from her mother, feeling sure that she would do what she promised, since her parents had made it a point never to make her a promise without fulfilling it. Time after time, she would say, "Promise me, Ma." To which, the mother would reply, "I do not like to make a promise to you, Mary, for fear I shall not fulfill it."

This request was urged at various times for nearly six years, and finally, the little petitioner had to die to secure the promise. Several times during her sickness, her parents came to her bedside to see her die. But she would say, "No, Ma, I can't die till you promise me."

Still, her mother was unwilling to make the promise, lest it should not be kept. She intended to give her heart to Jesus sometime but was unwilling to do it then.

Mary grew worse and finally uttered her last word on earth. Her mother was never again to hear that earnest entreaty, "Promise me, Ma." But the little one's spirit lingered, as if detained by the angel sent to lead the mother to Jesus, that the long-sought promise might be heard before it took its flight.

The weeping mother stood, watching the countenance of the dying child, who, with a look, seemed to be saying, "Ma, promise me, and let me go to Jesus!"

There was a great struggle in the mother's heart as she said to herself, *Why do I not promise this child? I mean to give my heart to Jesus; why not now? If I do not promise her now, I never can.*

The Spirit inclined her heart to yield. She roused the child and said, "Mary, I will give my heart to Jesus."

This was the last bolt to be drawn; her heart was now open. Jesus entered at once, and she felt the joy and peace of sins forgiven.

This change was so marked that she felt constrained to tell the good news to her child, that she might bear it with her when she went to live with Jesus. So, calling her attention once more, she said, "Mary, I have given my heart to Jesus, and He is my Savior now!"

For six years, Mary had been praying to God and pleading with her mother for these words. Now, as they fell on her ear, a peaceful smile lighted up her face.

No longer able to speak, she raised her pale little hand slightly and, pointing upward, seemed to say, "Ma, we shall meet up there." Her life's work was done, and her spirit returned to Him who gave it.

The mother's heart was full of peace, though her loved one had gone. But now she felt anxious that her husband should have this blessing that she found in Christ. The parents went together into the room where the dead child lay, to look upon the face of her who slept so sweetly in death. The mother then said, "I promised our little Mary that I would give my heart to Jesus, and He has received me. Now, won't you promise?"

The Holy Spirit was there. The strong man resisted for a while, then yielded his will. Taking the cold little hand in his, he knelt and said, "Jesus, I will try to seek Thee."

The child's remains were laid in the grave. The parents were found in the house of prayer—the mother happy in Jesus, and the father, too, soon having some evidence of love of Christ.

When I closed my labors in Springfield, Dr. Ide said to his congregation, "I hope you will all give Brother Earle some token of your regard for his services before he leaves." As this mother heard these words, she said she could, as it were, see her little Mary's hand pointing down from heaven and hear her sweet voice saying, "Ma, give him my two one-dollars."

Those two "one-dollars" I have now, wrapped around the picture of that dear child, and wherever I go, little Mary will speak for the Savior.

—Shaw, *Dying Testimonies of Saved and Unsaved*

As in the case of his friend John Calvin, no tombstone marks the place where this great reformer of Scotland is buried. When his body was laid in the grave, the Earl of Morton said, "Here lieth a man who in his life never feared the face of man."

Before dying, Knox said, "By the grace of God, I am what I am. Live in Christ, and the flesh need not fear death."

—Gottschall, *Selections from Testimonies and Dying Words*

# "I Have Treated Christ like a Dog All My Life"

About twenty years ago, when we were holding revival meetings, Mr. B—, a well-to-do farmer who lived nearby, was in the last stages of tuberculosis. He was a wicked man, all of his life having been spent in laying up treasures on earth. The pastor of a Methodist church whom we were assisting had not as yet called on him because he was so ungodly.

One day, the pastor said to me, "I am waiting until Mr. B— is near his end, hoping he will then allow me to talk to him about his soul."

Thus, several days before his death, in company with this pastor, we visited the man and talked with him about his moral condition. His mind was dark and full of unbelief. We talked earnestly with him about the saving of his soul but had to leave him without receiving much encouragement.

A day or two later, we called on him again and found him more willing to converse, but he still seemed to be far away from God. We pleaded with him, urging that he call on God to have mercy on him, for Jesus' sake.

"I cannot!" he cried. "I have never spoken the name of Jesus except when using it in profanity, and I have used it that way all of these years. I have treated Christ like a dog all of my life, and He will not hear me now. I would give all I am worth if I could only feel as you say you feel."

We told him that God was no respecter of persons and that He never turned any away who came to Him for pardon.

The farmer still resisted, saying, "I cannot get any feeling. What can I do? My heart is so hard."

Oh, how our hearts ached for him. He was afraid to die without faith in God, but he seemed to have no ability to repent.

Before we left the town, Mr. B— went to meet his God, unprepared, so far as we know, as he gave no evidence of salvation. He had treasures on earth, but, alas, that did not avail him anything when he came to face eternity.

How are you treating the Christ on whom you must depend if you are to be saved?

—Shaw, *Dying Testimonies of Saved and Unsaved*

# Sir Walter Raleigh (1618)

Just before being beheaded, this famous English admiral and courtier said to his executioner, "It matters little how the head lies if the heart be right. Why dost thou not strike?"

—Gottschall, *Selections from Testimonies and Dying Words*

# John Calvin (1564)

Reformist John Calvin's unremitting labors favored the inroads of a variety of distressing diseases, which he suffered from for many years, and against which he bravely battled or resolutely disregarded. He hated nothing so much as idleness.

On February 6, 1564, with difficulty, he preached his last sermon. After that, he left his house only a few times. In the midst of intense sufferings, his spirit was calm and peaceful, and he occupied himself with the Bible and with prayer.

When famed French evangelist William Farel, in his eightieth year and in fragile health himself, heard of Calvin's sickness, he wrote from Neuchâtel that he would pay a visit. Calvin replied in a letter dated May 2, 1564,

> Farewell, my best and most right-hearted brother, and since God is pleased that you should survive me in this world, live mindful of our friendship, of which, as it was useful to the church of God, the fruit still awaits us in heaven. I would not have you fatigue yourself on my account. I draw my breath with difficulty, and am daily waiting till I altogether cease to breathe. It is enough that to Christ I live and die; to His people He is gain in life and death. Farewell again—not forgetting the brethren.

On May 27, as the sun was setting, John Calvin fell asleep in Jesus. He was buried on the banks of the Rhône, outside the city where he had so long labored on behalf of the gospel of the Lord Jesus Christ. He asked that no monument be placed upon his grave. In fact, the spot where the black stone was erected is only conjectured to be his actual burial place.

Nineteenth-century Calvin scholar Dr. John Tulloch well said of Calvin, "He was a great, intense, and energetic character who, more than any other even of that great age, has left his impress on the history of Protestantism."

His clear intellect and his logical acumen, together with his concise and crisp style, make his works, even in the present day, a power in the church of God. He was needed in the church as truly as Luther, Knox, or Wesley, and we thank God for the gift of such a man.

—Shaw, *Dying Testimonies of Saved and Unsaved*

# Captain John Lee
# (1784)

Captain Lee was executed for forgery. He had been an infidel, but before his death, he said, "I leave to the world the mournful memento that however much a man may be favored by personal qualifications or distinguished mental endowments, his genius will be useless and his abilities avail little unless accompanied by religion and attended by virtue. Oh, that I had possession of the meanest place in heaven and could but creep into one corner of it!"

—Gottschall, *Selections from Testimonies and Dying Words*

# "I Am So Looking Forward to Seeing Jesus"

*Submitted by Hasula Hanna of Aurora, Colorado*

My husband, Homer, was a man very close to God. He often expressed a wish to be in the ministry but did not feel that was where God wanted him to serve. His was the quiet, personal ministry no one ever knew about, except Jesus and the one who was approached.

In the spring of 1951, he was having trouble with his stomach and thought he had ulcers. However, after a prolonged period, the distress persisted, so he went in for a checkup. The doctors told us that nothing definite showed up on the examination but that they wanted to perform exploratory surgery.

Our daughter, in her junior year at high school, was programmed for the lead in a music festival, and he postponed the surgery a week so he might hear her sing.

On March 27, he went into surgery for what the doctor thought would be a quick procedure. After waiting in the lounge for more than two hours, I began to feel that it was more involved than just minor surgery. When the doctor finally came to see me, I was told that they had found a perforation at the top of his stomach and that his lymph glands and other tissues showed some infection. They proceeded to remove most of the stomach, built a new elimination connection with the intestine, and were sending the removed organs to a cancer lab in Houston, Texas. The doctor added that he had no doubt the results would reveal a malignancy. He was right. The glands had been infected and had spread the sickness throughout my husband's body. It was a particularly virulent type that would not respond to any type of treatment then known. Doctors said that the cancer most likely would reoccur in the lungs within six to eight months—and would be terminal within two months after that.

Homer seemed to accept the prognosis much easier than I did. He began to heal and was able to accept food much sooner than the doctors expected. He regained his strength quickly, put on weight, and felt well. After his return to work on May 28, his coworkers and our friends even began to scoff at the idea that he had a limited time left.

However, some of the men whom he had tried to witness to prior to his illness came to him and asked how he felt about the prospect of limited life. This time, they were ready to listen to his declaration that life hereafter is surer than life here. His witness bore fruit many times.

By September, he began to tire easily, and a slight cough developed. His monthly X-ray showed a slight shadow on the lung, which became even larger by his next follow-up appointment. The doctor wanted to try radium in spite of the lab's verdict that the disease would not respond. They were correct; it didn't. Instead, it spread, and Homer went downhill rapidly. By the first week of November, he was unable to leave his bed, as the malignancy wrapped itself around the esophagus, making it hard to take solid food.

The men from work would drop in to cheer him up, but they would leave cheered themselves instead, for Homer expressed to them an actual expectancy at the prospect of seeing our Lord Jesus.

Mary, a close friend, came one evening in late November and said, "Homer, I know you believe in God's healing power. Have you asked to be healed?"

Homer's answer was simple and clear: "Mary, since I have come to feel that God has used this to reach people I had been unable to reach otherwise, I do not feel I have any right to ask Him to set aside His will. Instead, I am so looking forward to seeing Jesus; I would be disappointed if anything happened to prevent it."

The following Tuesday, he had a coughing attack, and the doctor suggested he get to the hospital. We went, and after we arrived, he told me, "Honey, never forget how much I love you!" Shortly after that, he fell into a coma, and within forty-eight hours, he went home to see his Lord.

As I tell this story, I want to thank God, for He was so merciful throughout the entire ordeal. At no time during his sickness did Homer suffer.

# Maggie Lindsay (1874)

Miss Lindsay was fatally injured in a railway collision in Scotland. After lying in the wreckage for several hours with both legs broken, her skull fractured, and other internal injuries, she was rescued at last and removed to a nearby cottage.

It was supposed she had been reading her much-loved hymn, "The Gate Ajar for Me," since that page of her hymnal was stained with her blood. Lying upon a stretcher with bleeding lips and dying breath, she sang the two following stanzas:

> Nothing, either great or small,
> Remains for me to do;
> Jesus died, and paid it all—
> Yes, all the debt I owe.[5]
>
> Oh, depth of mercy, can it be
> That gate was left ajar for me?
> For me? For me?
> Was left ajar for me![6]

—Gottschall, *Selections from Testimonies and Dying Words*

5. J. E. Gould, "Jesus Paid It All," 1869.
6. Lydia O. Baxter, "The Gate Ajar for Me," 1872.

# "It Was the Cursed Drink That Ruined Me"

To one of New York City's Bellevue hospital holding cells, there came one morning a woman bearing the usual permit to visit a patient. She was a slender woman with a look of delicate refinement that sorrow had only intensified. The physician was just leaving the patient as she approached. She looked at him with clear eyes that had wept often but kept their steady, straightforward gaze.

"I am not certain," she said. "I have searched for my boy for a long while, and I think this may be he. I want to see him."

The doctor looked at her pityingly as she went to the narrow bed where a lad of hardly twenty lay, his face buried in the pillow. His fair hair, curled crisply against skin browned by exposure, had not been cut, for the hospital barber, who stood there, found it so far impossible to make him turn his head.

"He's lain that way ever since they brought him in yesterday," said the barber, and then, moved by something in the agitated face before him, he turned his own way. The mother stooped over the prostrate figure. She knew it, as mothers seem always to know their own, and laid her hand on his burning brow.

"Charley," she said softly, as if she had come into his room to rouse him from some boyish sleep, "Mother is here."

The patient let out a wild cry that startled even the experienced physician.

"For God's sake, take her away! She doesn't know where I am. Take her away!" The patient had started up and wrung his hands in piteous entreaty. "Take her away!" he still cried, but his mother gently folded her arms about him and drew his head to her breast.

"Oh, Charley, I have found you," she said through her sobs, "and I will never lose you again."

The lad looked at her a moment. His beautiful, reckless face was graven with lines by passion and crime. He burst into weeping like a child.

"It's too late! It's too late!" he said, in tones almost inaudible. "I'm doing you the only good turn I've ever done you, Mother. I'm dying, and you won't have to break your heart over me anymore. It wasn't your fault. It was the cursed drink that ruined me, blighted my life, and brought me here. It's murder now, but the hangman won't have me—I'll save that much disgrace for our name."

As he spoke, he fell back upon his pillow. His face changed, and the unmistakable hue of death suddenly spread over his handsome features. The doctor came forward quickly, a look of anxious surprise on his face.

"I didn't know he was that bad," the barber muttered under his breath as he gazed at the lad, still holding his mother's hand. The doctor lifted the patient's head and then laid it back softly. Life had fled.

"It's better to have it so," the doctor said in a low voice, and then he stood silently, ready to offer consolation to the bereaved mother, whose face was still hidden on her boy's breast. She did not stir. Something in the motionless attitude aroused vague suspicion in the mind of the doctor and moved him to bend forward and gently take her hand. With an involuntary start, he lifted her prostrate form and quickly felt the pulse and heart, only to find them stilled forever.

"She has gone, too," the doctor softly whispered, and the tears stood in his eyes. "Poor soul! It is the best for both of them."

This is one story of the prison ward of Bellevue, and there are hundreds that might be told, though never one sadder or holding deeper tragedy than the one recorded here.

—Shaw, *Dying Testimonies of Saved and Unsaved*

# Louis IX
## (1270)

Louis IX, king of France, was noted not only for wisdom and justice but also for piety and virtue.

His dying advice to his daughter contained these words:

> My dear daughter,
>
> I conjure you to love our Lord with all your might, for this is the foundation of all goodness. I wish you could comprehend what the Son of God has done for our redemption. Never be guilty of any deliberate sin, though it were to save your life. Shun, too, familiar discourse, except with virtuous persons. Obey, my dear daughter, your husband. Aspire after a disposition to do the will of God, purely for His sake, independently of the hope of reward or the fear of punishment.

—Gottschall, *Selections from Testimonies and Dying Words*

# Queen Elizabeth I
## (1603)

Queen Elizabeth ascended the English throne at the age of twenty-five and remained in power for forty-five years. She was a Protestant but lived a lifestyle that was far from what anyone would consider that of a true Christian. She persecuted the Puritans for many years, and her cruelty was manifested throughout her reign.

We take the following from the *Schaff-Herzog Encyclopedia of Religious Knowledge* (1805):

> With Elizabeth, Protestantism was restored and—in spite of occasional resistance from within and the Spanish Armada and papal deposition from without—became the permanent religion of the large majority in the land.
>
> Two periods stand out in the history of the Church of England under Elizabeth. In the early part of the reign, the divorce of the national church from the Roman Catholic Holy See was consummated; in the latter part, its position was clearly stated in regard to Puritanism, which demanded recognition, if not supremacy, within its pale.

The queen was no zealous reformer but directed the affairs of the church with the keen sagacity of a statesmanship, which placed national unity and the peace of the realm above every other consideration. In the first year of her reign, the Acts of Supremacy and the Act of Uniformity were passed. By the former, all allegiance to foreign prince or prelate was forbidden; by the latter, the use of the liturgy was enforced.

Her royal title of Defender of the Faith and Supreme Head of the Church was retained, with the slight alteration of "Head" to "Governor." But the passage was struck out of the litany that read, "From the tyranny of the Bishop of Rome and all his detestable enormities, good Lord, deliver us."

The queen retained, against the protests of bishops, an altar and crucifix, and lighted candles in her own chapel. She disapproved of the marriage of the clergy, interrupted the preacher who spoke disparagingly of the sign of the cross, and imperiously forced her wishes upon unwilling prelates.

She died in 1603 at the age of seventy. Her last words were, "All my possessions for a moment of time!"

—Shaw, *Dying Testimonies of Saved and Unsaved*

# Raymond Lull
## (1315)

While seeking to convert the Muslims, Raymond Lull was stoned by a mob in the North African city of Bougie. Although he managed to board a vessel, he died from the injuries he had received. His parting words were as follows:

> I was once rich, lascivious, and worldly, but willingly did I forsake everything to advance the glory of God and the good of mankind. I learned Arabic and departed to preach to the Saracens.

For my religion, I have been whipped and imprisoned. Now, I am old and poor yet steadfast in the same purpose, and through grace, steadfast will I remain.

—Gottschall, *Selections from Testimonies and Dying Words*

# Matthew Henry
# (1714)

On the return journey from a visit to Chester, England, Matthew Henry, a distinguished nonconformist and biblical scholar, was seized with apoplexy. His old, intimate friend, Mr. Illidge, was present, who had been desired by Sir Thomas Delves and his lady to invite him to their house at Doddington. Unable to proceed any further, they stopped at Mr. Mottershed's house, where Henry felt himself so ill that he said to his friends, "Pray for me, for now I cannot pray for myself."

While they were putting the great scholar to bed, he spoke of the excellence of spiritual comforts in a time of affliction and blessed God that he enjoyed them. To his friend Mr. Illidge, he addressed himself in these memorable words: "You have been used to take notice of the sayings of dying men. This is mine: That a life spent in the service of God and communion with Him is the most comfortable and pleasant life that one can live in the present world."

—Shaw, *Dying Testimonies of Saved and Unsaved*

# Hannah More
# (1833)

Hannah More was an English religious author and philanthropist. As she neared death, an unusual brightness came over her face, followed by a smile. She reached out her arms, as if grasping something.

"Joy!" she exclaimed, then was gone. Joy was the name of a sister who had died some years previously.

—Gottschall, *Selections from Testimonies and Dying Words*

# "You Cannot Run Away from the Spirit of God"

*Submitted by Mary E. Jenks of McBain, Michigan*

Several years ago, a gentleman, apparently in great haste, entered a certain city in one of the Southern states on horseback. He rode to the hotel, alighted, and, after introducing himself, told the following story:

> I have been trying to run away from the Spirit of God, but it has followed me all of these many miles that I have traveled, and it is with me now. I had Christian training and, as I heard the gospel proclaimed from time to time, became deeply convicted of sin. However, I was very rebellious and determined not to yield. The Spirit said, "You must be born again," but I said, "I will not be born again."

> I purchased this horse—a good, strong beast at the time—and I have worn it down poor, as you see; but I have not succeeded in outrunning the Spirit of God. I feel that I am about to die, and I have a request to make. I want you to sell this horse and bury me here in the street by this signpost. Put up a slab by my grave bearing this inscription: "You cannot run away from the Spirit of God."

The man soon died. Physicians examined him and said there was no disease about him; he died of mental agony.

His strange request was granted, and the slab bearing this silent warning preached many a sermon to passersby, resulting in a revival of religion in the city of Tuscaloosa, Alabama.

—Shaw, *Dying Testimonies of Saved and Unsaved*

# A Young Woman Looks into Eternity

One of the predecessors of my last pastorate was Rev. A. D. Sandborn, who related the following incident. He was president of a school at Wilton, Iowa, and, while going back and forth to his school, he would usually stop for a few moments of conversation with a devoted young Christian woman who was seriously ill.

One morning, he found the family gathered at her bedside. She was bolstered up nearly in a sitting position and was intently looking off into the distance. She seemed to see a glorious city, for she said, "Now, just as soon as they open the gate, I will go in. They will be here very soon now."

As she looked, her eyes just danced. Suddenly, she leaned her head forward with a happy, eager expression. "There! There!" she said. "They are coming now, and I shall go!" Then, she sank back upon her pillow with a disappointed look and exclaimed, "They have let Little Mamie in ahead of me." Then, she added, "But next time they will let me in. Pretty soon they will open the gate again, and then I will go in."

Still gazing eagerly and expectantly into space, she lay quietly for a few minutes. Then, starting up with head leaning forward and eyes straining to see, she exclaimed, "There! There! They are going to open the gate. Now I shall go in!"

Again, however, she sank back on the pillows in sore disappointment. "They let Grandpa in ahead of me—but next time, I will go in for sure. They will be back pretty soon."

She still kept looking far away and talking. No one spoke to her, and she said nothing to anyone in particular. She seemed to see nothing save for the sights of the beautiful city.

Dr. Sandborn could not remain from his duties longer and quietly left the house. Later in the day, he learned that the woman had died soon after he had left the house. She died just as he had seen her, so full of eager expectancy and waiting for the gate to open and give her entrance into the beautiful city.

The scenes of that morning made a profound impression on Dr. Sandborn, and a few days after the funeral, he called at the house to inquire who it was that the dying girl had called "Little Mamie." Her family told him that Mamie was a little girl who had lived near them at one time. Later, she had moved to a town in New York. To his question "Who was Grandpa?" they replied that he was an old friend of the young lady and that he had moved to some place in the Southwest.

All of the circumstances made such an impression on Dr. Sandborn that he wrote to each of the postmasters in the places referred to, asking for information on these people.

One day, in the same mail, he received letters from the two postmasters replying to his questions. Both letters were worded very much alike, and in each instance, the letter stated that the person referred to had lived there but had died on the morning of September 16, naming the hour. This proved to be the same time that he had witnessed that affecting deathbed scene.

—Judson B. Palmer, *The Child of God: Between Death and the Resurrection*

# William Otterbein (1813)

Bishop Otterbein, founder of the United Brethren Church, ended a ministry of sixty-two years in great peace.

Dr. Kurtz of the Lutheran Church, for many years a devoted personal friend of the distinguished preacher, offered at his bedside the last audible prayer. The bishop responded, "Amen, amen! It is finished." Like good old Simeon, who was spared to take the babe of Bethlehem in his arms, he could say, *"Lord, now lettest thou thy servant depart in peace, according to thy word: for mine eyes have seen thy salvation"* (Luke 2:29–30).

His grief-stricken friends, thinking at that moment that he was dying, gathered around him to take the last look, but, rallying again, as if to finish his testimony and give still greater assurance of victory, Otterbein said, "Jesus, Jesus, I die, but Thou livest, and soon I shall live with Thee."

Then, turning to his friends, he continued, "The conflict is over and past. I begin to feel an unspeakable fullness of love and peace divine. Lay my head upon my pillow and be still."

All was then quiet. He simply awaited the approach of heaven's chariot, and he did not wait in vain. A smile, a fresh glow, lighted up his countenance; and, behold, it was death.

—Shaw, *Dying Testimonies of Saved and Unsaved*

# Anne Askew
## (1546)

Anne Askew was an English poet and a Protestant who was condemned to die as a heretic. She is the only woman on record to have been both tortured in the Tower of London and burned at the stake.

Because of her adherence to the Protestant faith, her husband had driven her violently from their home, even though she was the mother of his two children. While imprisoned, an apostate named Nicholas Shaxton advised her to recant. She replied by telling him that it would be well had he never been born.

Being placed upon the cruel rack, her joints and bones were pulled out of place. After recovering from a faint, she preached to her tormentors for two hours. On the day of her execution, she had to be carried on a chair, her bones being so dislocated that she could not walk.

After she had been fastened to the stake with a chain, a letter was brought offering pardon from the king if she would recant. While in the midst of the flames, Anne Askew died praying for her murderers. Her last recorded words, an answer to the king's offer of pardon, were these: "I came not thither to deny my Lord and Master."

—Gottschall, *Selections from Testimonies and Dying Words*

# Bishop William Hanby
## (1880)

Bishop William Hanby, a devoted preacher of the United Brethren Church, began to weep shortly before he died. His daughter noticed this and tenderly inquired, "What is it, Father?"

"Oh, I am so happy," was his reply. "My long, toilsome journey is nearly ended; my life work is joyfully over; half of my children are already safe in heaven, and I am just as sure the rest will be. Half are safe at home, and all the rest are on the way. Mother is there, and in a little while, I shall be there, too!"

Then, he quoted the following hymn:

> The Lord My Shepherd is,
> I shall be well supplied.
> Since He is mine and I am His,
> What can I want beside?[7]

After he had descended into the river, he suddenly shouted back, "I'm in the midst of glory!"

—Shaw, *Dying Testimonies of Saved and Unsaved*

# Agrippina the Younger
# (59)

*Mother of the Roman Emperor Nero*

This infamous ruler once had a female rival beheaded for imperial dignity. The head being brought to her, she examined it closely with her own hands in order to be sure it was the one she wanted.

She was eventually condemned to death by her own son, Emperor Nero. To the men sent to slay her, she said, "Strike here! Level your range against the womb which gave birth to such a monster!"

—Gottschall, *Selections from Testimonies and Dying Words*

7. Isaac Watts, "The Lord My Shepherd Is," 1719.

# "Too Late! Too Late! Too Late!"

*Submitted by J. Earnest of Searcy, Arkansas*

When I lived in west Tennessee, I was well acquainted with a noted infidel who neither feared God nor regarded man. He considered it an insult to his dignity for anyone to speak to him on the subject of religion. In fact, he had been known to fight some who dared approach him about his soul's salvation. Although he had been favored with an abundance of the earthly possessions of this life, it seemed to me that he was the most unhappy man that I had ever seen.

When this man was dying, his weeping sister asked her husband, who also was a rough man and an infidel, to go get my uncle so that he might pray for her brother. Of course, my uncle responded, and when he entered the room, the dying infidel said to him, "I can now see and realize that I am doomed to hell. Pray for me!"

Uncle did all he could. I was along, and while Uncle was praying and singing, I tried to keep the man's mind on the Lord by talking to him.

Nothing seemed to help, however, and the poor fellow kept warning all present not to live as he had lived and sink at last to a devil's hell. Finally, he turned his face toward the wall and, with an awful wail, cried, "Too late! Too late! Too late!"

—Shaw, *Dying Testimonies of Saved and Unsaved*

# Oliver Cromwell
# (1658)

The devil is ready to seduce us, and I have been seduced."

—Gottschall, *Selections from Testimonies and Dying Words*

# Me

Me was an old, blind warrior of the South Sea Islands. He had a plantation on which he raised sweet potatoes and bananas, but when he was stricken with disease, others seized his property. A missionary found him alone and suffering from the pangs of hunger.

The old warrior said, "I am not lonely, for I have frequent visits from God. God and I were talking when you came in."

—Gottschall, *Selections from Testimonies and Dying Words*

# A Victory Crossing

I'll see you in the morning."

Those were the last words William G. Roll spoke to me, shortly before he passed from time into eternity. Although we had been loath to let him go—hoping the Lord's will might permit him to remain among us for yet a longer time—he had whispered, "My body is weary; I would like to go home." Then, with a flash of his delightful smile, he repeated his farewell: "I'll see you in the morning."

In those few words was a world of faith, trust, and hope, as well as an eagerness to be gone to meet his Savior. There was no uncertainty and no fear, just a deeply settled peace and unbounded confidence.

Nor were there any tears or regrets. His life in God's service, his triumphant passing, savors of the words of the apostle Paul: *"I have fought a good fight, I have finished my course, I have kept the faith"* (2 Timothy 4:7).

For the first time in the history of the fellowship, eternity has reached out to enfold a member of our International Board. We feel a great sense of loss. We shall miss his voice in our councils; his steady, unwavering faith in difficult days, as well as his prayers and his hold on God for the Fellowship and its work. But what an abundant entrance for him!

Our brother Roll has contributed more than any other one man to building the truly international stature of the Full Gospel Business Men's Fellowship International. For years a diplomatic representative of the United States in foreign courts, he has opened numerous doors in many nations, through which we have been able to carry the gospel into areas that otherwise might not have been available to us.

Though his earthly voice is now silent, he yet speaks to us through our memory of his faith and service.

—Demos Shakarian, *Full Gospel Business Men's Voice,* March 1967

# Philip Melanchthon (1799)

Philip Melanchthon's ever ready pen, clear thought, and elegant style made him "the scribe of the Reformation." His last known words, in answer to his son-in-law's question as to whether he wanted anything, quoted from John 1:10, 12:

*"'The world knew him not....But as many as received him, to them gave he power to become the sons of God, even to them that believe on his name.'* I want nothing but heaven, therefore trouble me no more."

—Gottschall, *Selections from Testimonies and Dying Words*

# David Nelson (1844)

David Nelson, a noted Presbyterian clergyman, was born on September 24, 1793. In 1810, he graduated from Washington College, in Virginia, and he practiced medicine for some years. Several of these years he spent as a surgeon in the United States Army. It was during this period that he became an infidel.

In the providence of God, however, his eyes were opened, and he was saved from his "refuge of lies." Thrilled with newfound faith and love for God, Mr. Nelson began to preach in the spring of 1825. Five eventful years of serving the Lord in Tennessee and Kentucky were climaxed with God's call to go to Missouri and establish Marion College. He was the school's first president, a position he held for six years.

Then, in 1836, he opened a training school for missionaries, and in the succeeding years, he wrote a widely circulated book, *The Cause and Cure of Infidelity.*

Mr. Nelson died in 1844, and his last words were, "My Master calls; I am going home. It is well."

—Shaw, *Dying Testimonies of Saved and Unsaved*

# Edward Augustus
# (1820)

*Duke of Kent and Father of Queen Victoria*

In the prospect of death, Augustus's physician strove to soothe his mind by referring to his honorable conduct. The duke stopped him, saying, "No. Remember, if I am to be saved, it is not as a prince but as a sinner."

—Gottschall, *Selections from Testimonies and Dying Words*

# "I Am Going to Die. Glory Be to God and the Lamb Forever!"

These were the last words of the saintly Ann Cutler, one of John Wesley's workers in whom he had great confidence. She was converted under the famed William Bramwell, who wrote the following account:

> Ann Cutler was born near Preston, in Lancashire, in 1759. Until she was about twenty-six years of age, though very strict in her morals and serious in her deportment, she never understood the method of salvation by Jesus Christ. Then, the Methodist local preachers visited that neighborhood. After hearing one of them, she was convinced of sin and from that time gave all diligence to obtain mercy.

In a short time, she received pardon, and her new life evinced the blessing she enjoyed. It was not long, however, before she had a clearer insight into her own heart, and, though she retained her confidence of pardon, she became sensitive to the need of perfect love. Upon hearing the doctrine of sanctification and believing that the blessing is to be received through faith, she expected instantaneous deliverance and prayed for the power to believe. Her confidence increased until she could say, "Jesus, Thou wilt cleanse me from all unrighteousness!"

In the same year of her finding mercy, she found a sinking into humility, love, and dependence upon God. At this time, her language was, "Jesus, Thou knowest I love Thee with all my heart. I would rather die than grieve Thy Spirit. Oh, I cannot express how much I love Jesus!" After this change, something remarkable appeared in her countenance: there was a smile of sweet composure. It was noticed by many as a reflection of the divine nature, and it increased to the time of her death.

In a few months, she felt a great desire for the salvation of sinners and often wept much in private, drawn out to plead with God for the world in general. She would frequently say, "I think I must pray; I cannot be happy unless I cry for sinners. I do not want any praise. I want nothing but souls to be brought to God. Though reproached by most, I cannot do it to be seen or heard of men. I see the world going to destruction, and I am burdened till I pour out my soul to God for them."

Her great devotion to God is shown in the following account of her sickness and death by Mrs. Highfield:

> I will endeavor to give you a few particulars relative to the death of Ann Cutler. While she was with us, it seemed to be her daily custom to dedicate herself, body and soul, to God. She came to Macclesfield very poorly of a cold on the fifteenth of December. Being [that it was] our preaching night, she had an earnest desire to have a prayer meeting. I told her that on account of preaching lasting so late as eight o'clock, and the classes having to meet afterwards, it would not be convenient.
>
> She was very importunate, however, and said she could not be happy without one. "I shall not be long here, and I would buy up every opportunity of doing something for God—time is short."

Knowing she had an uncommon talent for pleading for such souls as were coming to God, we got a few together, to whom she was made a blessing.

A few days before her death, she said, "Jesus is about to take me home. I think I shall soon have done with this body of clay; and, oh, how happy shall I then be when I cast my crown before Him, lost in wonder, love, and praise!"

About seven a.m., the doctor, with those of us about her, thought she was gone, but, to our great surprise, she continued in an unconscious state till between ten and eleven o'clock. She then lifted herself up and looked about her, speaking so as to be heard. She was very sensible and seemed perfectly composed, but her strength was nearly gone.

Finally, about three o'clock, she looked at her friends and said, "I am going to die." Then, she added, "Glory be to God and the Lamb forever!" These were her last words. Soon afterwards, the spirit left this vale of misery.

—Shaw, *Dying Testimonies of Saved and Unsaved*

# The Sad Death of a Lost Man

In Texas, there lived a wealthy farmer, the son of a Methodist preacher. He was highly respected in the community in which he lived and was a kindhearted and benevolent man. However, he had one great fault. He was very profane. He would utter the most horrible oaths, seemingly without the least provocation.

Several times, I remember having seen him under deep conviction during revival meetings. On one occasion, when under powerful conviction during a camp meeting, he said he was suddenly frightened and felt as if he wanted to run away from the place. He was again brought under conviction, but he refused to yield.

Shortly after this, he was suddenly taken ill and died in three days. I was with him in his last moments. He seemed to be utterly forsaken of the Lord from the beginning of his sickness. The most powerful medicines had no effect on him whatsoever, and, just as the sun of a beautiful Sunday morning rose in its splendor over the eastern hills, he died in awful agony.

All through the night prior to his death, he had suffered untold physical and mental torture. He offered the physicians all his earthly possessions if they would save his life, but he was stubborn and would not acknowledge his fear of death until a few moments before he passed. Then, suddenly, he began to stare into the vacancy before him. Horribly surprised and frightened, he exclaimed, "My God!"

The indescribable expression of his countenance at this juncture, together with the despairing tones in which he uttered these last words, made every heart quake. His wife screamed and begged a brother to pray for him, but the brother was so terror-stricken that he rushed out of the room. The dying man continued to stare in dreadful astonishment, his mouth wide open, till at last, with an awful groan,

> Like a flood with rapid force,
> Death bore the wretch away.[8]

His three-year-old son, the idol of his father's heart, was convulsed with grief. This little boy, then so innocent, grew up to be a wicked young man and died a horrible death.

How solemn to reflect that in hell, there are millions of fathers and sons, mothers and daughters, husbands and wives, hopelessly lost.

Realizing that the future state of those who know not God will never abate its fury but, in accordance with the natural law of sin, degradation, and wretchedness, will grow worse and more furious as the black ages of eternity roll up from darker realms, we turn for relief to the Man of Sorrows, who tasted death for every man. Then, we turn to the beautiful city whose Builder and Maker is God, to the bliss of the glorified, who will shine as the stars forever and ever. Then, with renewed efforts, we continue with gratitude to work out our own salvation, and the salvation of others, with fear and trembling.

—Shaw, *Dying Testimonies of Saved and Unsaved*

8. Isaac Watts, "My Thoughts on Awful Subjects Roll," 1834.

# Monsieur Homel
## (1683)

Monsieur Homel was a French Protestant pastor who was martyred in 1683. Almost every bone of his body was broken with the iron bar of the wheel upon which he had suffered for forty hours before the executioner gave him a death blow upon the breast.

Before dying, he said, "Farewell, my dear wife. I know that your tears and your continual sighs hinder you from bidding me adieu. Do not be troubled at this wheel upon which I must die. It is, to me, a triumphal chariot which will carry me into heaven. Farewell once more, my well-beloved spouse. I am waiting for you. But know, though you see my bones broken to shivers, my soul is replenished with inexpressible joys. I see heaven opened and Jesus with His outstretched arms!"

—Gottschall, *Selections from Testimonies and Dying Words*

# John Oxtoby
## (1830)

John Oxtoby, one of the great men of Methodism, was soundly converted to Christ in 1804 after spending many years of his life in sin. Soon after his conversion, he began to preach the gospel, and thousands of lives were transformed as a result of his ministry.

His biographer, Harvey Leigh, gives the following account:

> That which gave lasting effect to the labors of John Oxtoby was the uncommon power of the Spirit which attended his words. Seldom did he

open his mouth, either in preaching, praying, or personal conversation, without those being addressed feeling the force of that unction.

Not infrequently during his preaching have numbers of people actually fallen to the ground crying for mercy, under the most striking apprehensions of their sin and danger. Others, who with great difficulty escaped home, were impelled to send for him or others to pray for them before they dared attempt to sleep. And, strange as it may seem, some have even fallen to their knees on their way home, and others at their work, from the effects of his preaching and prayers.

During the whole of the affliction which brought about his death, he had a most glorious experience of God's favor. He received such a baptism of the Holy Spirit that his soul was filled with peace and joy unutterable. Amidst the sinkings of mortality, he approached the vale of death as if "prayer was all his business, and all his pleasure, praise."

A little while before his departure, he said, "As great as have been my comforts from the Lord during the years of my life, yet all the former manifestations which I have had are nothing compared with those which I now feel."

To his sister, he said, "Oh, what have I beheld! Such a sight as I cannot possibly describe. There were three shining forms beside me whose garments were so bright and whose countenances were so glorious that I never saw anything to compare with them before!"

His dying prayer was, "Lord, save souls; don't let them perish." Shortly afterward, he shouted in holy triumph, "Glory, glory, glory!" and immediately soared on high.

—Shaw, *Dying Testimonies of Saved and Unsaved*

# "Lost! Lost! Lost!"

The following incident concerns a young lady who, under deep conviction of sin, left a revival meeting to attend a dance arranged by a party of ungodly men in an attempt to break up the revival. She caught a severe cold at the dance and before long was on her deathbed.

When a local minister visited her, she stiffly repulsed his efforts to counsel her, saying, "Mr. Rice, my mind was never clearer. I tell you all today that I do not wish to be a Christian. I don't want to go to heaven; I would not if I could. I would rather go to hell than heaven; they need not keep the gates closed."

"But you don't want to go to hell, do you, Jennie?" the minister implored.

She then broke down and replied, "No, Mr. Rice. Oh, that I had never been born! I am suffering now the agonies of the lost. If I could but get away from God. But no, I must always see Him and be looked upon by Him. How I hate Him; I cannot help it! I drove His Spirit from my heart when He would have filled it with His love, and now I am left to my own evil nature—given over to the devil for my eternal destruction. My agony is inexpressible! How will I endure the endless ages of eternity? Oh, the dreadful thought of eternity!"

When asked by Mr. Rice how she got into this despairing mood, she replied, "It was that Friday evening last winter when I deliberately stayed away from the meeting to attend the dance. At the dance, I felt so sad, for my heart was tender; I could scarcely keep from weeping. Yet I felt provoked to think that my last dance, as I somehow felt it to be, should be spoiled by these feelings. I endured it until I became angry; then, with all my might, I drove the influence of the Spirit away from me. It was then that I had the feeling that He had left me forever. I knew that I had done something terrible, but it was done. From that time, I have had no desire to be a Christian but have been sinking down into deeper darkness and more bitter despair. And now, all around and above and beneath me are impenetrable clouds of darkness. Oh, the terrible gloom; when will it cease?"

She then sank away and lay like one dead a short time. Finally, she raised her hand slightly, her lips quivering as if in the agonies of death. Suddenly, her eyes opened with a fixed and awful stare, and she gave a despairing groan that sent chills through every heart.

"Oh, what horror!" she whispered.

Then, turning to Mr. Rice, she said, "Go home now; return this evening. I don't want you to pray for me. I don't want to be tormented with the sound of prayer."

About four o'clock, she inquired the time and, upon being told, exclaimed, "How slowly the hours wear away. This day seems an age to me. Oh, how will I endure eternity?" In about an hour, she again said, "How slowly the time drags. Why may I not cease to be?"

That evening, she sent for Mr. Rice again. As he approached her bed, she said to him, "I want you to preach at my funeral. Warn all of my young friends; remember everything I have said, and use it."

"How can I do this? Jennie, how I do wish you were a good Christian and had a hope of eternal life."

"Now, Mr. Rice, I don't want to hear anything about that. I do not want to be tormented with the thought. I am utterly hopeless; my time is growing short; my fate is eternally fixed! I am dying without hope because I insulted the Holy Spirit so bitterly. He has just left me alone to go down to eternal night. He could not have borne with me any longer and retained His divine honor and dignity."

Soon after that, she began to struggle in the agonies of death. She gasped, "Oh, save me! They drag me down! Lost! Lost! Lost!"

A moment later, she rallied and, with glazed eyes, looked upon her weeping family and friends for the last time. Her eyelids sank partly down and pressed out a remaining tear as she whispered the strange yet knowing words, "Bind me, ye chains of darkness! Oh, that I might cease to be, but still exist."

The spirit fled, and Jennie Gordon lay a lifeless form of clay.

—Shaw, *Dying Testimonies of Saved and Unsaved*

# "I Didn't Know It Was So Beautiful"

The following is an excerpt from *Hulda: The Pentecostal Prophetess* by Byron J. Rees (1898):

> Hulda A. Rees was a successful evangelist of the Society of Friends. She was born October 15, 1855, and lived only forty-two years, but her life had made an impact upon her generation.

We saw the end approaching from a distance, but we could not fully realize the truth. It did not seem like *"the valley of the shadow"* (Psalm 23:4). We had read of the triumph of the saints when approaching the river, but, surely, this excelled anything of which we had ever heard. Such sweet resignation to all God's will, such divine unction in prayer, such holy tenderness in exhortation and admonition, such victory and gladness in the furnace of pain and agony!

Many visitors came to see her, and, whenever her strength permitted, she always had them admitted to her room. Her words were ever full of cheer and eternal hope. On one occasion, when a minister called whom she had known for years, she said to him with the greatest exultation, "The glory holds!"

Yes, thank God, it did hold. The gospel she had preached to so many thousands with emphasis and assurance was found true and unshakable in this time of earnest testing.

In one of her prayers, she said, "Thou hast put, O Lord, a great laugh in my heart. Glory! Glory be to Thy name forever! No evil can come to me! All is turned to blessing!"

One afternoon, the family was all gathered about her when, suddenly, her face lighted up as if a candle were burning beneath the transparent skin. With the brightest, sweetest smile and a faraway look as if she were gazing off in the distance, she said in a soft, reflective tone, "I didn't know it was so beautiful."

Then, after a moment or so, she exclaimed rapturously, "Can it be that the glory of the Lord is risen upon me?"

Thus, this daughter of the Most High drew near to the exit from this world. It was indeed to her, as she said, "All bright and glorious ahead."

The night before she ascended, she attempted to sing:

> Fear not, I am with thee;
> O be not dismayed!
> For I am thy God,
> And will still give thee aid.[9]

9. Robert Keen, "How Firm a Foundation," 1787.

But she could only whisper the words. Her husband read the entire hymn to her.

On the evening of Friday, June 3, as the darkness was deepening about us, we watched her slip quietly away. There was no struggle. She passed away from us as calmly as a child falling asleep. We knew that she was with the Lord, both hers and ours.

—Shaw, *Dying Testimonies of Saved and Unsaved*

# A Dying Man's Regrets

A minister once said to a dying man, "If God should restore you to health, do you think that you would alter your course of life?"

The man answered, "I call heaven and earth to witness, I would labor for holiness as I shall soon labor for life. As for riches and pleasure and the applause of men, I account them as dross. Oh, if the righteous Judge would but reprieve and spare me a little longer, in what spirit would I spend the remainder of my days! I would know no other business; I would aim at no other end than perfecting myself in holiness. Whatever contributed to that—every means of grace, every opportunity of spiritual improvement—should be dearer to me than thousands of gold and silver. But, alas! Why do I amuse myself with fond imaginations? The best resolutions are now insignificant because they are too late!"

Such was the language of deep concern uttered by one who was beginning to look at these things in the light of the eternal world, which, after all, is the true light.

Here we stand on the little molehills of earthly life, where we cannot get a clear view of that other world; but what must it be to stand on the top of the dark mountain of death and look out upon our surroundings, knowing that, from the top of that mountain, if angels do not lift us to the skies, we must take a leap into the blackness of darkness!

—Shaw, *Dying Testimonies of Saved and Unsaved*

# Rev. Thomas Walsh (1759)

Thomas Walsh is a great name in the history of early Methodism. Both preacher and scholar, he mastered not only his native Irish language but also was versed in Latin, Greek, and Hebrew. It is said that he studied so deeply that his memory was an entire concordance of the whole Bible.

His soul was as a flame of fire. John Wesley said of him, "I do not remember ever to have known a man who, in so few years as he remained upon earth, was the instrument of converting so many sinners."

The ministry of Walsh was mostly in Ireland, and the Roman Catholic priests simply could not account for the extraordinary influence he possessed. Preaching on mountains and highways, in meadows, private houses, prisons, and ships, he bore down all before him by a kind of absorbed ecstasy of ardent faith.

Dying at the early age of twenty-seven, he suddenly became oppressed with a sense of despair, even to doubting his own salvation. The sufferings of his mind were protracted and very intense, but, at last, he broke through and, just before the end, exclaimed, "He is come! He is come! My Beloved is mine, and I am His—forever!"

—Shaw, *Dying Testimonies of Saved and Unsaved*

# "There Is Light All Around Me!"

*A noted evangelist of the nineteenth century, Mrs. Grace Weiser Davis wrote this account of her mother's beautiful passing in* The Christian Standard, *published July 10, 1898.*

For five months past I have been a witness to the triumphs of the power of God to save amid suffering and to cast out all fear that hath torment.

My mother left us July 20 at the age of fifty-nine. She and my father were converted just previous to my birth in a revival that continued for almost a year. After that, our home was always open to ministers of the gospel. Mother would give them the best she could get and then apologize because it was no better. Hundreds can testify to her loving ministrations.

When her last sickness came, we brought her to Bradley Beach, hoping for a prolongation of the precious life. She was cheerful, planning for a continued life here, and we shrank from telling her the truth. God Himself, however, gloriously revealed it to her. The doctor and other ministers bear testimony with my own that hers was the most glorious deathbed we had ever witnessed.

One day, my mother prayed, "Dear Lord, prepare me for the country to which I am going!" Before the close of that day, she was shouting the praises of God. From that time on, she talked of her coming translation, and her faith was gloriously triumphant.

On Sunday, June 27, she had a day of wonderful exaltation. She said, "I have always hoped and trusted in God, but now I have a fuller realization than ever before." As we all wept, she said, "I don't realize that this is death. It is His will, and is all right." To the doctor, she said, "Just think, Doctor, to be forever with the Lord!"

After that, no one could come into Mother's room without being spoken to about the glory that was filling her soul. To me, she said, "Grace, God has given you gifts that few others possess. Let us pray that God will make you a weight of glory in the world. God has blessed you and will still more."

One afternoon, she said, "I am homesick for heaven." To the doctor, she said, "Sometimes my way has seemed dark, but it was like the Ferris wheel—it always came round to a point of light."

Again, she said, "I believe I will awake sometime and find myself in a strange country, to which I shall be translated."

"Mother, it will not be so strange," I answered. "Your father and mother and husband and little boy are there, and we are on the way."

To one lately married, she said, "You are just beginning life. It pays to begin right. Everything you'll do for God is on interest—*compound* interest. It will be doubly repaid you. I commenced to serve Him in early life and consecrated my children to Him in infancy, and they are all Christians, and I am so happy."

As I kissed her one day, she said, "We shall rejoice together in Jesus in heaven." Her favorite words were, *"Surely goodness and mercy shall follow me all the days of my life: and I will dwell in the house of the* L*ORD for ever"* (Psalm 23:6). Her favorite hymn was "Jesus, Lover of My Soul."

The night previous to her death, she said, "There is light all around me!"

Until the last, she gave evidence of hearing, seeing, and understanding. I knelt within fifteen minutes of her passing and said, "Mother, though you walk through the valley of the shadow of death, you need fear no evil, for God is with you. Surely goodness and mercy shall follow you, and you are going to dwell in the house of the Lord forever."

There came a responsive smile. In a few minutes, she drew a gentle breath and was gone.

—Shaw, *Dying Testimonies of Saved and Unsaved*

# Phillip J. Jenks

Just before Phillip J. Jenks passed away, a friend asked, "How hard is it to die?"

"I have experienced," Jenks replied, "more happiness in two hours today, when dying, than in my whole life. I have long desired that I might glorify God in my death, but I never thought that such a poor worm as I could come to such a glorious death."

—Gottschall, *Selections from Testimonies and Dying Words*

# George Edward Dryer (1896)

*This young saint of God went to heaven from Readsburg, Wisconsin, on February 1, 1896. His sister, Mrs. Evaline Dryer Green, wrote the following:*

Dear readers, come with me for a little while as I look on memory's walls. See, there are many things written there! Here is one story, sweet and sacred—almost too sacred to relate—yet, as with hushed voices we talk of this, our hearts shall melt, and we shall feel that heaven is drawing nigher.

I remember my baby brother, though I was a child of but four years when he came into our home. I well remember that little face and the chubby brown hands when he was a wee boy—always in mischief then. I was a frail girl, and he soon outgrew me. Then, those sweet years of home life and, later, the glad homecomings when I was away at school. On my return, George was always the first to wave his hand and shout for joy. Often, he would toss his hat high in the air and give a certain "whoop" and three cheers, which I loved to hear. We were right loyal friends, my brother and I.

But then it struck. Ah, it's here I'd wish to draw the veil and forget. He was so strong, so full of life! But we will only glance at those long months of suffering and hasten to the last. Nearly eighteen months of weariness from coughing, and there he lay, the picture of patient endurance, saying from his heart's depths,

> Farewell, mortality, Jesus is mine,
> Welcome, eternity, Jesus is mine![10]

Often, he would call me near him and say, "Oh, sister, the Lord does so save me!"

To the doctor, to the boys of his own age, to his neighbors, and to all who came, he testified of how Jesus had saved him, through and through.

The last hours were drawing near. One of the Lord's servants came and prayed. George prayed for father, mother, brothers, and sisters. Later in the evening, a

10. Jane C. Bonan, "Jesus Is Mine," 1843.

sweat, deathly cold, covered him. We thought he was going then—the poor, weak body seemed all but gone—but the spirit grew even more bright. Ah, that picture! His high, marble-white brow, either cheek glowing with fever intense; the great, expressive blue eyes that peered earnestly, joyfully, all about him and upward.

Then, with heaven lighting his face, he lifted those dear hands high and said, "Angels now are hovering round us!"

Even now, I shall say, as I did then, "'*O death, where is thy sting? O grave, where is thy victory?*'" (1 Corinthians 15:55).

Again he came back to us to spend one more night of suffering on earth and one more night working for God and eternity. We watched all night while he praised God, often saying under his breath, between awful fits of coughing, "Precious Jesus!"

Toward morning, he asked a dear sister to sing "I Saw a Happy Pilgrim."

Finally, the morning came, a dark, rainy February day. The gray light was just dawning when we all gathered about his bed. We repeated beautiful texts and verses of hymns that he most loved and encouraged him to the very river's brink. His last spoken words were, "Eva, come on this side."

Then, peacefully, he closed his eyes and grew so still.

> And with the morn, those angel faces smile,
> Which I have loved long since and lost awhile.
>
> —John Henry Newman

—Shaw, *Dying Testimonies of Saved and Unsaved*

# Jessie

Little Jessie's mother was dying. Her last words to the child were "Jessie, find Jesus!"

After the funeral, Jessie began, in her simple, childlike way, to obey her mother's request. As a young man came out of a saloon and almost stumbled over her, she asked, "Please tell me where Jesus Christ is."

"I don't know, child," he replied.

On one occasion in her wanderings, she met a Jewish woman, of whom she asked, "Do you know Jesus Christ?" The woman turned fiercely upon her and exclaimed, "Jesus Christ is dead!"

Finally, one day, a rough boy snatched her little basket and threw it into the street. While she was endeavoring to regain it, the horses of a passing streetcar trampled her underfoot. The doctors said she could not live till morning, but during the night, she suddenly opened her eyes, and her face lit up with a glad smile. Just before her lips were hushed in death, she said, "Oh, Jesus, I have found You at last!"

—Gottschall, *Selections from Testimonies and Dying Words*

# Rev. John S. Inskip
## (1884)

*Adapted from John E. McDonald,* The Life of Rev. John S. Inskip *(1885)*

This great evangelist of full salvation was greatly used in bringing Christians from a life of wandering in the wilderness of doubts and fears to the "Promised Land" of perfect rest. For many years, he was at the head of the great holiness movement in America. His biographer wrote, "The agents whom God uses for special work are marked men—men who seem, by special enduement, to be leaders; and who at once, by their superior adaptation, command public attention and take their place, by general consent, in the front ranks. Such a character was Rev. John S. Inskip."

He was a great sufferer for many weeks before he died. On one occasion, Mrs. Inskip said, "My dear, religion was good when you were turned from your father's home; it was good in the midst of labor, trials, and misrepresentations; it has been good in the midst of great battles; and, when the glorious victory came, does it now hold in the midst of this great suffering?"

He pressed her hand and, with uplifted eyes and a hallowed smile, responded, "Yes, oh yes! I am unspeakably happy." This was followed by, "Glory! Glory!"

During his sickness, he requested many of his friends to sing and pray with him. He was always cheerful, his face radiant with smiles and bright with the light of God. The last song sung on the day of his departure was "The Sweet By-and-By." While singing that beautiful and appropriate hymn, the dying man pressed his loving wife to his breast, and then, taking her hands in his, raised them up together and, with a countenance beaming with celestial delight, shouted, "Victory! Triumph! Triumph!" These were his last words on earth.

He ceased to breathe at 4 p.m., March 7, 1884, but so peacefully and imperceptibly did he pass away that those who watched by him could scarcely perceive the moment when he ceased to live. On that day the Christian warrior, the powerful preacher, the tender husband, the world-renowned evangelist, was gathered to his fathers and rested from his toil.

—Shaw, *Dying Testimonies of Saved and Unsaved*

# Claudius Salmasius
# (1653)

*A Distinguished French Classical Scholar*

I have lost a world of time! Had I one year more of life, it would be spent in pursuing David's psalms and Paul's epistles. I would mind the world less and God more."

—Gottschall, *Selections from Testimonies and Dying Words*

# The Child Martyr

*Noted evangelist E. P. Hammond supplied the following reliable and very touching article for this work:*

I have been surprised to notice how many children have died a martyr's death rather than deny Jesus. I want to tell you about one of these young martyrs. In Antioch, where the disciples were first called Christians, a deacon from the church of Caesarea was called to bear cruel torture meant to force him to deny the Lord, who had bought him with His precious blood. While suffering, he still declared his faith, saying, "There is but one God and one mediator between God and man, Christ Jesus."

His body was almost torn into pieces. The cruel emperor Galerius seemed to enjoy looking upon him in his suffering. At length, this martyr begged his tormentors to ask any Christian child whether it was better to worship one God—the maker of heaven and earth—and one Savior—who had died for us and was able to bring us to God—or to worship the many gods whom the Romans served.

There stood nearby a Roman mother who had brought with her a little boy nine years of age, that he might witness the sufferings of this martyr from Caesarea. The question was asked of the child, who quickly replied, "God is one, and Christ is one with the Father."

The persecutor was filled with fresh rage and cried out, "Oh, base and wicked Christian, that you have taught this child to answer thus." Then, turning to the boy, he said more mildly, "Child, tell me, who taught you thus to speak? Where did you learn this faith?"

The boy looked lovingly into his mother's face and said, "It was God that taught it to my mother, and she taught me that Jesus Christ loved little children, and so I learned to love Him for His first love for me."

"Let us see what the love of Christ can now do for you," cried the cruel judge. At a sign from him, the officers who stood by with their rods quickly seized the boy and made ready to torture him.

"What can the love of Christ do for him now?" asked the judge, as blood began to stream from the tender flesh of the child.

"It helps him," cried the mother, "to bear what his Master endured for him when He died for us on the cross."

Again, they smote the child, and every blow seemed to torture the agonized mother as much as the boy. As the blows, faster and heavier, were laid upon the bleeding boy, they again asked, "What can the love of Christ do for him now?"

Tears fell from heathen eyes as that Roman mother replied, "It teaches him to forgive his tormentors."

The boy watched his mother's eye and no doubt thought of the sufferings of his Lord and Savior. When his tormentors asked if he would now serve the gods they served, he still answered, "I will not deny Christ. There is no other God but one, and Jesus Christ is the Redeemer of the world. He loved me and died for me, and I love Him with all my heart."

The poor child at last fainted between the repeated strokes, and they cast the torn and bleeding body into the mother's arms, supposing that he was dead.

"See what the love of Christ has done for your Christian boy now!"

As the mother pressed him to her heart, she answered, "That love will take him from the wrath of man to the peace of heaven, where God shall wipe away all tears!"

But the boy had not yet passed over the river. Opening his eyes, he said, "Mother, can I have some water from our cool well upon my tongue?"

His eyes were closing in death when the mother answered, "Already, dearest, thou hast tasted of the well that springeth up unto everlasting life. Farewell! Thy Savior calls for thee. Happy, happy martyr! For His sake may He now grant thy mother grace to follow in thy bright path."

To the surprise of all, after they thought he had breathed his last, he again raised his eyes and looked to where the elder martyr was. In almost a whisper, he said, "There is but one God, and Jesus Christ whom He has sent."

With these words upon his parched lips, the child passed into God's presence, where "*is fullness of joy*" (Psalm 16:11), and to His right hand, where "*there are pleasures for evermore*" (verse 11).

—Shaw, *Dying Testimonies of Saved and Unsaved*

# "I Can See the Old Devil Here on the Bed with Me"

*How shall we escape, if we neglect so great salvation...?* (Hebrews 2:3–4)

At one time, there lived in our neighborhood a man whom we will call Mr. B—. He was intelligent, lively, a good conversationalist, and had many friends. But Mr. B— loved strong drink and was not friendly to Christianity. He would not attend church and would laugh and make fun of religion. Some of his neighbors he called "Deacon So-and-so" for fun. But Mr. B— was growing old, and his head was frosted over with many winters. He had long since passed the age of seventy.

At the close of a wintry day, in a blinding snowstorm, a neighbor called at our home saying that Mr. B— wished to see my husband. Knowing Mr. B— was ill, my husband was soon on his way. On entering the sickroom, he asked Mr. B— what his wishes were.

"Oh, I want you to pray for me," he replied.

"Shall I not read a chapter from the Bible to you first?"

Mr. B— assented, and the chapter selected was the fifth chapter of John. While my husband was reading, Mr. B— would say, "I can see the old devil here on the bed with me, and he takes everything away from me as fast as you read it to me. There are little ones on each side of me."

After the reading, prayer was offered for him, and my husband urged him to pray for himself.

"I have prayed for two days and nights and can get no answer," the older man answered. "I can shed tears over a corpse, but over this Jesus I cannot shed a tear. It is too late, too late! Twenty-five years ago, at a camp meeting held near my home, that was the time I ought to have given my heart to Jesus.

"Oh," he cried, "see the stream coming up! See the river rising higher and higher! Soon it will be over me, and I will be gone."

The room was filled with companions from other days, but not a word was spoken by them. Fear seemed to have taken hold, as one said, "I never believed in a hell before, but I do now. Oh, how terrible!"

Mr. B— lived but a short time after that. He died as he had lived, a stranger to Jesus, with no hope in His cleansing blood.

—Shaw, *Dying Testimonies of Saved and Unsaved*

# "For This Has Been His Kingdom"

*Through the kindness of Dr. L. B. Balliett of Allentown, Pennsylvania, comes the following incident:*

A boy lay dying of his wounds in one of the hospitals during the Civil War. Realizing his near end, a Christian nurse asked, "Are you ready to meet your God, my dear boy?"

The large, dark eyes opened slowly, and a smile passed over the young soldier's face, as he answered, "I am ready, dear lady, for this has been His kingdom." As he spoke, he placed his hand upon his heart.

"Do you mean," questioned the lady gently, "that God rules and reigns in your heart?"

"Yes," he whispered, then passed away. His hand still lay over his heart after it had ceased to beat.

—Shaw, *Dying Testimonies of Saved and Unsaved*

# Andronicus
## (393)

The martyr Andronicus, after being imprisoned, was most cruelly scourged, and his wounds rubbed with salt. Later, he was brought out and tortured again, thrown to wild beasts, and afterward killed with a sword.

"Do your worst; I am a Christian," he had said before his execution. "Christ is my help and supporter, and, thus armed, I will never serve your gods—nor do I fear your authority, or that of your master, the emperor. Commence your torments as soon as you please. Make use of every means that your malignity can invent, and you shall find in the end that I am not to be shaken from my resolution!"

—Gottschall, *Selections from Testimonies and Dying Words*

# Frances E. Willard
## (1898)

*The following is adapted from Anna A. Gordon and Lady Henry Somerset,* The Beautiful Life of Frances E. Willard *(1898)*

On the last day God let us have Frances with us, Mrs. Hoffman, the national recording secretary of our society, entered the room for a moment. Miss Willard seemed to be unconscious, but, as Mrs. Hoffman quietly took her hand, she looked up and said, "Why, that's Clara, good Clara! Clara, I've crept in with Mother, and it's the same beautiful world and the same people. Remember that—it's just the same."

A few moments later, a message of tender solicitude and love was received from dear Lady Henry. As I read the precious words, I heard Miss Willard's voice: "Oh, how sweet; oh, how lovely, good—good!"

Quiet as a babe in its mother's arms, she fell asleep, and, though we knew it not, the dew of eternity was soon to fall upon her forehead. She had come to the borderland of this closely curtained world.

Only once more did she speak to us. About noon, her thin, white hand—that active, eloquent hand—was raised in an effort to point upward, and we listened for the last time on earth to the voice that, for thousands of people, had surpassed all others in its marvelous sweetness and magnetic power. She must have caught a glimpse of that other world for which she longed, for she said, in tones of utmost content, "How beautiful it is to be with God!"

As twilight fell, hope died in our yearning hearts, for we saw that the full glory of another life was soon to break o'er our loved one's earthly horizon. Kneeling about her bed with the faithful nurses who had come to love their patient as a sister, we silently watched while the life immortal—the life more abundant—came in its fullness to this dear soul, whose cherished wish from her youth—that she might go, not like a peasant to a palace, but as a child, to her Father's home—was about to be fulfilled.

Slowly, the hours passed with no recognition of the loved ones about her. Then, there came an intent upward gaze of her blue eyes, a few tired sighs, and, at the "noon hour" of the night, Frances Willard was...

> Born into beauty
> And born into bloom,
> Victor immortal
> O'er death and the tomb.

—Shaw, *Dying Testimonies of Saved and Unsaved*

# Sudden Death

*Submitted by Julia E. Strail of Portlandville, New York*

At one time, during a prayer meeting, my attention was directed toward an unsaved lady who was present and who appeared to be trifling. The pastor in charge of the meeting made the remark that as a watchman upon the walls of Zion, he felt that there was danger for someone there. He could not understand why he was impressed with this thought, and he repeated that he felt drawn out to say that there was danger and someone there ought to get saved, then and there.

This irreligious lady appeared unconcerned and oblivious to his remarks; she laughed when the minister shook hands with her at the close of the meeting. However, just as she was preparing to leave the church, she was taken very ill—so ill that she could not go home, and neither could she be taken home by friends. Everything that could be done for her relief was done, but, in less than one short hour, she passed into eternity.

Before she died, she tore her hair, cast aside the trashy ornaments that adorned her person—of which she had been very fond—and, throwing up her hands, cried aloud for mercy: "Oh, Lord, have mercy on me! Oh, Lord, help me!"

In this distress of body and soul, she passed into eternity, without leaving any hope to those that stood around her dying form.

This sad experience is a striking illustration of the danger of putting off the day and hour of salvation. *"For in such an hour as ye think not the Son of man cometh"* (Matthew 24:44).

—Shaw, *Dying Testimonies of Saved and Unsaved*

# John Hus
# (1415)

*Famous Bohemian Martyr*

The great Bohemian reformer and martyr, John Hus, was born in 1369. He was burned at the stake as a heretic on July 6, 1415, in Constance, Germany.

When arriving at the place of execution, he prayed, "Into Thy hands, O Lord, do I commit my spirit. Thou hast redeemed me, O most good and faithful God. Lord Jesus Christ, assist and help me that, with a firm and present mind, by Thy most powerful grace, I may undergo this most cruel and ignominious death to which I am condemned for preaching the truth of Thy most holy gospel."

After the wood was piled up to his neck, the Duke of Bavaria asked him to recant.

"No," said Hus, "I never preached any doctrine of an evil tendency, and what I taught with my lips, I now seal with my blood."

It is also recorded that Hus said, "You may cook the goose today, but God shall raise up a gander, and him, you'll never roast!" *Hus,* in Bohemian, means "goose," whereas *Luther* is derived from the German word for *gander.* Luther was not even born at this time.

The fagots were then lighted, and the martyr sung a hymn so loud as to be heard through the crackling of the flames.

—Shaw, *Dying Testimonies of Saved and Unsaved*

# William Pitt
# (1778)

*English Statesman and First Earl of Chatham*

I have, like other men, neglected spiritual matters too much to have any ground of hope that can be efficacious on a deathbed. However, I now throw myself on the mercy of God, through the merits of Christ."

—Gottschall, *Selections from Testimonies and Dying Words*

# Rev. J. M. Morris
# (1891)

Rev. J. M. Morris was born February 15, 1807, in Campbell County, Virginia, and died when he was nearly eighty-four years old, February 4, 1891, at Mores Creek, California.

When Morris was twelve, his father died, leaving him as the main support of his mother. He had had only thirty days' schooling, all told, at that time. By the aid of shell bark hickory as a substitute when out of candles, he devoted his evenings to study. He went through English grammar and arithmetic, and partially through advanced algebra, without a teacher. As a grown man, he was rarely surpassed in sound biblical learning and doctrine.

In early life, he was deprived of attending church and Sunday school, but he was impressed with the necessity of a change of heart. We give his experience in his own words:

> When a lone boy, having hardly ever heard anyone pray or preach, while all alone in the cotton field, with my hoe in hand, I became powerfully convicted that I was a sinner. I tried to pray as best I could, and the Lord came down in mighty power and blessed my soul. I did not know what to do or say, but God put it into my mind to praise His name; so, there, with hoe in hand and both arms outstretched, I shouted, "Glory to God!" All looked beautiful. The sun and sky never looked so bright as when I was alone in that cotton patch with no one near but God.

In meetings, Morris became "shouting happy" while relating this experience, and the holy fire would spread. Everyone went home saying, "We had a good meeting; Morris was in the cotton patch today."

In 1857, he crossed the plains with oxen teams to Trinity County, California. Going into a hotel near the mines, he demolished the saloon where the grog was sold and preached for two years in the barroom, as it was called, where a class (church) of twenty-five or thirty was formed.

Though he preached and labored as colporteur (a distributor of religious books) in California for nearly thirty years, he crossed the plains three times with oxen teams, four times by rail. During these trips, he preached in Iowa, Missouri, and Kansas.

Disposing of all his little earthly effects in his last sickness, he said, "I die in peace with all men; I shall soon be with the angels. All I want is to be a little twinkling star."

On calling Mother Morris, he said, "The other day, you came to my bed and said, 'I want you to get well and pray as you used to once.' I have not been able to pray since, and I shall never be any better, but I want you to write to all the grandchildren and tell them I'd rather leave this request of their grandmother as a legacy to them than all the gold of Ophir."

He made us promise that we would bury him in a plain coffin on the farm where he had lived for twelve years. No flowers or parade were to be given in his honor.

For thirty days, we watched, day and night, taking four persons each night. All agreed that they did not know that anyone was capable of suffering so much as he did, but his patience and resignation held fast. He would say, "I am in the hands of the great God of the universe; He knows best." Often, he would pray, "Oh, help me to be patient. The will of the Lord be done."

After suffering from asthma, lung trouble, and something like the grippe, for thirty days, he drew his last breath, just as if he were going to sleep, in his right mind and without a struggle or a groan.

—Shaw, *Dying Testimonies of Saved and Unsaved*

# Probus (304)

Accused of being a Christian, Probus was scourged until the blood flowed, loaded with chains, and consigned to prison. Some days later, he was brought out and commanded to sacrifice to the heathen gods.

"I come better prepared than before, for what I have suffered has only strengthened me in my resolution. Employ your whole power upon me, and you will find that neither you, nor the emperor, nor the gods you serve, nor the devil who is your father, shall compel me to worship idols!"

After much further torture and imprisonment, he was finally killed with the sword, but his resolution held firm.

—Gottschall, *Selections from Testimonies and Dying Words*

# He Saved His Face and Lost His Soul

*Submitted by Rev. Thomas Graham*

A young man by the name of Smith was seen looking on with interest during a prayer service at a camp meeting in Rootstown, Ohio. One of the ministers noticed him and spoke to him on the subject of his salvation. His eyes filled with tears, and he seemed inclined to seek Christ.

One of his wicked companions, however, perceived this and stepped up. "Smith, I would not be a fool."

Poor Smith could not resist such influences. Dashing the tears from his eyes, he turned on his heel and went away.

He lingered about the campground until the meeting closed and then went off with his company. They bantered him on the subject of his feelings. To show them that he had not the feelings they supposed, he commenced cursing and blaspheming in a most awful manner, making all imaginable sport of religious things.

Suddenly a large tree limb fell on him, and, without one moment's warning—and with a curse on his tongue—he was forced into the presence of the God, whom he had thus been blaspheming.

—Shaw, *Dying Testimonies of Saved and Unsaved*

# "You Will Let Me Die and Go to Hell"

*Submitted by Rev. E. G. Murrah*

Mr. H—, a wealthy planter in South Carolina around the year 1860, had come to his dying hour. He had made this world his god and used his influence and money against the cause of Christianity. When the last hour approached, he felt that he was a ruined man and requested his wife—who was as sinful as he was—to pray for him.

"I can't do it," she replied. "I don't know how. I never prayed in my life."

"Well," he said, "send for one who is a Christian to pray for me."

"For whom shall I send?" she asked.

"Send at once for Harry, the coachman. He is a man of God."

"No," she replied, "I'll never do that. It would be an everlasting disgrace to have a Negro pray for you in your house."

"Then you will let me die and go to hell before you will suffer a Negro to pray for me!"

And she did.

*Pride goeth before destruction, and an haughty spirit before a fall.*
(Proverbs 16:18)

—Shaw, *Dying Testimonies of Saved and Unsaved*

# "I Can Now Die Happy"

*A Young Woman Wins Her Lover to Christ at the Last Moment*
*As told by Rev. C. P. Pledger of Chicago, Illinois*

Addie Asbury was dying. The doctor said that she could not live but a short time, perhaps only minutes. She called her friends to her bedside and, one by one, bade them good-bye, asking them to meet her in heaven.

All at once, she opened her eyes and said, "I want to see Tom."

She had been engaged to marry a man named Tom for several years but would not marry him because he was not a Christian. Being told that he was not there, she insisted that she had a message for him, whereupon she was assured that Tom would be sent for.

Knowing that she had but a short time and that Tom lived quite a distance away, her friends doubted whether he would arrive before she died. Seeming to read their thoughts, she said, "The God that I have loved and served can keep me here until he comes. I have a message for him, so please send at once."

We went for him, and although fully an hour elapsed before we returned, she was still alive and waiting. At once, she reached out and took him by the hand, saying, "Tom, I want you to be a Christian. I am going to leave you, and I want to know before I go that you are a child of God."

"Why, Addie," said he, "I can't say that I am a Christian when I am not. I would like to be, but I can't."

Then, she took her Bible and showed him from its sacred pages that he could be if he would repent and believe on the Lord Jesus Christ, who could forgive his sins. Right then and there, the miracle took place. He accepted God's Word and opened his heart to the Savior. What a blessed sight it was!

After bidding all good-bye once more, the dying saint closed her eyes and murmured, "I can now die happy. Soul, take thy flight!"

A few years later, we saw Tom ordained a deacon in a Presbyterian church not far from where his betrothed had died. He is now one of the pillars of the church and is a faithful defender of the cause of Jesus Christ.

—Shaw, *Dying Testimonies of Saved and Unsaved*

# John Randolph
# (1833)

*American Orator and Statesman*

Remorse! Remorse! Remorse! Let me see the word—show it to me in a dictionary; write it on paper. Ah! Remorse! You don't know what it means! I cast myself on the Lord Jesus Christ for mercy!"

—Gottschall, *Selections from Testimonies and Dying Words*

# Thomas Paine (1809)

Thomas Paine was born at Thedford, England, in 1737. He is widely known for his connection with the American and French revolutions and for his infidel writings.

In 1791, he published *The Rights of Man*. In 1793, while in a French prison, he wrote *The Age of Reason*, his famous work against both atheism and Christianity and in favor of Deism. In 1802, he returned to the United States, where, as Adam Storey Farrar wrote, he "dragged out a miserable existence, indebted in his last illness for acts of charity to disciples of the very religion that he had opposed." Paine died in 1809.

We quote from McIlvaine's *Evidences of Christianity*:

> Paine's first wife is said to have died by ill usage. His second wife was rendered so miserable by neglect and unkindness that they separated by mutual agreement. His third companion, not his wife, was the victim of his seduction while he lived upon the hospitality of her husband.
>
> Holding a place in the excise of England, Paine was dismissed for irregularity; restored and dismissed again for fraud, without recovery. Unable to get employment where he was known, he came to this country, commenced as a politician, and pretended to some faith in Christianity. Congress gave him an office, from which, being soon found guilty of a breach of trust, he resigned in disgrace.
>
> The French Revolution allured him to France. Habits of intoxication made him a disagreeable inmate in the American minister's house, where, out of compassion, he had been received as a guest. During all this time, his life was a compound of ingratitude and perfidy, of hypocrisy and avarice, of lewdness and adultery. In June 1809, the poor creature died in this country.

The Roman Catholic bishop Edward Fenwick said,

A short time before Paine died, I was sent for by him. I was accompanied by F. Kohlmann, an intimate friend. We found him at a house in Greenwich (now Greenwich Street, New York), where he lodged. A decent-looking elderly woman came to the door and inquired whether we were the Catholic priests, "For," said she, "Mr. Paine has been so much annoyed of late by other denominations calling upon him that he has left express orders to admit no one but the clergymen of the Catholic Church." Upon [our] informing her who we were, she opened the door and showed us into the parlor.

"Gentlemen," said the lady, "I really wish you may succeed with Mr. Paine, for he is laboring under great distress of mind ever since he was told by his physician that he cannot possibly live and must die shortly. He is truly to be pitied. His cries when left alone are heartrending. 'O Lord, help me!' he will exclaim during his paroxysms of distress; 'God, help me! Jesus Christ, help me!'—repeating these expressions in a tone of voice that would alarm the house. Sometimes, he will say, 'O God! What have I done to suffer so much?' Then, shortly after, 'But there is no God'; and then, again, 'Yet, if there should be, what would become of me hereafter?' Thus he will continue for some time, when on a sudden, he will scream as if in terror and agony and call for me by my name. On one occasion, I inquired what he wanted. 'Stay with me,' he replied, 'for God's sake! I cannot bear to be left alone.' I told him I could not always be in the room. 'Then,' said he, 'send even a child to stay with me, for it is a hell to be alone.' I never saw a more unhappy man. It seems he cannot reconcile himself to die."

Such was the conversation of the woman, who was a Protestant and who seemed very desirous that we should afford him some relief in a state bordering on complete despair. Having remained for some time in the parlor, we at length heard a noise in the adjoining room. We proposed to enter, which was assented to by the woman, who opened the door for us.

A more wretched being in appearance I never beheld. He was lying in a bed sufficiently decent in itself but, at present, besmeared with filth. His look was that of a man greatly tortured in mind, his eyes haggard, his countenance forbidding, and his whole appearance that of one whose better days had been but one continued scene of debauch. His only nourishment was milk punch, in which he indulged to the full extent of his weak state. He had partaken very recently, as the sides and corners of his mouth exhibited traces of it, as well as of blood, which had also followed in the track and left its mark on the pillow.

Upon our making known the object of our visit, Paine interrupted, "That's enough, sir, that's enough. I see what you would be about. I wish to hear no more from you, sir! My mind is made up on that subject. I look upon the whole of the Christian scheme to be a tissue of lies, and Jesus Christ to be nothing more than a cunning knave and impostor. Away with you and your God, too! Leave the room instantly! All that you have uttered are lies, filthy lies, and if I had a little more time I would prove it, as I did about your impostor, Jesus Christ."

Among the last utterances that fell upon the ears of the attendants of this dying infidel, and which have been recorded in history, were the words, "My God, my God, why hast Thou forsaken me?"

—Shaw, *Dying Testimonies of Saved and Unsaved*

# The Last Words of Dr. Wakeley

*Submitted by Bishop Janes of the Methodist Church*

The deathbed scene of this saintly man was in harmony with his life experience. Taken suddenly and violently ill, Dr. Wakeley was composed amid his acute sufferings and without alarm as to the issue. When the doctors informed him they had no hope of his recovery, he received the information without agitation and continued tranquil and happy.

I have seen many Christians die happily, but I have never witnessed such perfect naturalness in the face of death. He conversed and acted in the same manner, with the same tone of voice, the same pleasant countenance, and the same cheerful spirit that had characterized him in health. In his sickness, from first to last, everything he said and did was perfectly "Wakeleyan." It did not seem like a death scene. It appeared more like the breaking of morning and the advancing of the day than the approach of evening and the gathering of the night shadows.

At my first interview with him, Dr. Wakeley said, "The doctors tell me there is no hope of my recovery; but I can say with Paul, '"*I am now ready to be offered, and the time of my departure is at hand. I have fought a good fight, I have finished my course, I have kept the faith*"' (2 Timothy 4:6–7)."

Then, he added, "I see my crown and mansion and inheritance."

"Yes," I said, "but you must die to possess them."

Instantly, he quoted the old hymn, "By death I shall escape from death and life eternal gain."[11]

At another time, he said, "I have fought long, fought honorably, fought heroically, fought successfully, fought for God, fought for Jesus, fought for Methodism, fought for Christianity. I have not gained all I wished, but, through Christ, I have taken great spoils."

He quoted from John 11:25–26: "'*I am the resurrection, and the life: he that believeth in me, though he were dead, yet shall he live: and whosoever liveth and believeth in me shall never die.*'" Looking at me earnestly, he said, "'*Believest thou this?*'"

"With all my heart," I said.

He responded, with much emotion, "So do I!"

Then, lifting up his hand, he quoted from liturgy, "The head that once was crowned with thorns is crowned with glory now; a royal diadem adorns the mighty Conqueror's brow. The spiritual kingdom of Christ in the earth is a mighty one. It must be set up in all the earth. It will over all prevail."

A few hours before his death, I asked him, "What shall I say to your brethren in the ministry?"

"Preach the Word!" was his firm reply. "Be instant in season, out of season—reprove, rebuke, exhort, with all long-suffering and doctrine." He repeated the words "with all long-suffering and doctrine" three times.

After a moment's rest while panting for breath, he added, "Tell them to preach the old gospel—we want no new one. It cannot be improved on. One might as well attempt to improve a ray of sunshine while vivifying a flower. The grand old gospel forever!"

11. James Montgomery, "Forever with the Lord," 1835.

He then said, "I leave all with God. I want it distinctly understood that I do so without any fear, without any cowardice, without any alarm. I do it with the boldness of an old soldier, and with the calmness of a saint."

He added, "They will inquire in the morning, 'Is Brother Wakeley dead?' Dead? No! Tell them he is better and alive forevermore!"

I said, "Yes, and a higher and nobler life."

He replied, "Wonderfully enlarged! Oh, wonderfully enlarged! I know the old ship. The Pilot knows me well. He will take me safe into port. Heavenly breezes already fan my cheeks. I shall not be a stranger in heaven. I am well-known up there. Like Bunyan, I see a great multitude with white robes, and I long to be with them. '"*To depart, and to be with Christ...is far better*"' (Philippians 1:23). When you go to the grave, don't go weeping. Death hath no sting. The grave hath no terror. Eternity hath no darkness. For many years, neither death nor the grave had any terrors for me. Sing at my funeral: 'Rejoice for a brother deceased; our loss is his infinite gain.'[12]

"Listen! Hear ye not the song? Victory is ours! There is great rejoicing in heaven. Roll open, ye golden gates, and let my car go through!"

Then, he added, "I must wait until the death angel descends."

Soon the death angel came, the silver cord was loosed, and his freed spirit ascended to glory and to God.

—Shaw, *Dying Testimonies of Saved and Unsaved*

# John Randon (1775)

John Randon was a British soldier who fell at the Battle of Bunker Hill. He said, "Bright angels stand around the turf on which I lie, ready to escort me to the arms of Jesus. Bending saints reveal my shining crown and beckon me away. Yea, Jesus bids me come! Adieu!"

—Gottschall, *Selections from Testimonies and Dying Words*

12. John Wesley Harding, "Rejoice for a Brother Deceased," year unknown.

# Cardinal Wolsey (1530)

Thomas Wolsey, one of the most distinguished men during the reign of King Henry VIII, was born in 1471. When he became chaplain to the king, he had many opportunities to gain royal favor. These he used to the utmost. He successively obtained several bishoprics and, at length, was made archbishop of York, lord high chancellor of England, prime minister, and, for several years, the arbiter of Europe.

The Holy Roman Emperor, Charles V, and the French king, Francis I, courted his interest and loaded him with favors. With immense revenues and unbounded influence, his pride and ostentation were carried to the greatest height. He had eight hundred servants, among whom were several lords, fifteen knights, and forty esquires.

From this great height of power and splendor, he fell into complete ruin. His ambition to become pope, his pride, his exactions, and his opposition to King Henry's divorce occasioned his disgrace. Such a great reverse affected his mind and brought on a severe illness, which soon put an end to his days.

A short time before he died, after reviewing his life and the misapplication of his time and talents, he sorrowfully declared, "Had I but served God as diligently as I have served the king, He would not have given me over in my gray hairs. But this is the just reward that I must receive for my incessant pains and study, not regarding my service to God, but only to my prince."

—Murray, *Power of Religion on the Mind*

# Charles M. de Talleyrand (1838)

When dying, this French statesman was asked by King Louis how he felt. He replied, "I am suffering, sire, the pangs of the damned!"

—Gottschall, *Selections from Testimonies and Dying Words*

# "He's Here in This Room, All Around Me"

*A noted evangelist of the last century, Rev. E. P. Hammond, supplied the following experience:*

A lady from Brooklyn, New York, has just sent me a most touching story about a cousin of hers, only nine years old. I could scarcely keep the tears from my eyes while reading it. This little boy's praying mother had been called to part with five of her children. This, her youngest, she dearly loved, and, when he showed signs of having learned to trust and love the dear Jesus, she loved him all the more. I will let you read a part of this kind lady's letter, just as it was read to me:

> One Sunday evening last spring, he was left alone with his older sister, whose husband had died a few weeks before. After endeavoring to comfort her in various ways, he suddenly said, "Sister, have you heard me tell a lie for a long time? I used to tell a great many, but I don't think I have now for six months, and I don't think God will let me tell any more. I don't want ever to do another wrong thing."

When he went to bed that night, she heard him pray that God would soon make him fit for those mansions that eye had not seen nor ear heard about.

On Thursday of that week, he went to get some fireworks with two other boys, that he might "amuse sister" on the Fourth of July. The railway train was going very slowly up a long hill, and, for fun, the boys stepped off the back platform and onto the front one. Charley slipped and fell, and the wheel of the carriage passed directly over his hip, crushing the bone to powder. He uttered one scream and never complained again.

When a policeman lifted him from his dreadful position, he opened his eyes and said, "Don't blame anybody; it was my fault. But tell my mother I'm going right to my Savior."

In telling of this later, the policeman said, "We all felt that there must be some reality in that boy's religion."

The sad news was told to his mother by two street children, who expressed it in these terms: "Does Charley live here? Well, he's smashed."

She followed the children and literally tracked her child to the hospital by his blood. When she entered the room where he lay, he opened his eyes and said, "Mother, I'm going to Jesus, and He's here in this room, all around me. Oh, I love Him so much! Don't let them cut off my leg; but, if they do, never mind. It won't hurt me as much as Jesus was hurt."

When his father arrived, he said, "Papa, I am going to my Savior. Tell my brother Eddy, that if he feels lonely now because he has no brother, to learn to love Jesus. He will be his Brother and love him so much."

These were the last words he said, for in about two hours, he bled to death. The hospital nurse was deeply touched and, as she closed his eyes, said, "He has gone to that Savior he talked so much about—and I will try to love Him, too."

When his mother returned home, her only words were, "The Lord has taken my Charley. '*Though he slay me, yet will I trust in him*' (Job 13:15)."

—Shaw, *Dying Testimonies of Saved and Unsaved*

# Clarence Darrow (1938)

I was interested to read a syndicated newspaper column by a medical doctor who claimed that even Clarence Darrow, the famed agnostic lawyer, was troubled in his soul as he lay on his deathbed.

"Get me three clergymen," Darrow said to his law clerk.

When the ministers arrived, Darrow, who had laughed at the Bible beliefs of William Jennings Bryan during the heated Scopes trial in Tennessee, said, "Gentlemen, I have written and spoken many things against God and the churches during my lifetime. Now, I wish I hadn't! For I realize it is entirely possible that I may have been wrong. So, I should like to ask a final favor: that each of you intercede with the Almighty for me."

The ministers did pray for Clarence Darrow, and I trust that he himself prayed the sinner's prayer.

—Haven of Rest Ministries radio program, *Log of the Good Ship Grace*, Vol. 33, No. 14, 1967

# A Reproof from the Scaffold

In 1877, in Newark, New Jersey, a young man was hanged for murder. Just before the fatal hour, he spoke to the people about him, saying, "If, in my early life, I had received one-half the attention and care from the good people of this city that has been shown me since this trial commenced, I should never have been a murderer."

A few years ago, we held a meeting in a certain Illinois town. Two men had met their death on the scaffold just before our meetings commenced, and the excitement of the event had not yet died away. We were told that two of the most prominent pastors of the city had shown considerable interest in these young men before they were executed. They visited the condemned men often, talking and praying with them. Both of them professed to be saved before they died.

One of the doomed men exhorted the people from the scaffold to take warning by his example and urged them to seek the Lord before they became guilty of some sin that would cause them and their families disgrace.

If the interest of Christians had been brought to bear upon these criminals before their crime, they might have been saved in their youth.

—Shaw, *Dying Testimonies of Saved and Unsaved*

# "Here She Is, with Two Angels with Her"

*Adapted from Laura Smith Haviland,* A Woman's Life Work *(1887)*

One day on the street, I met a Sister White who was much distressed about her son. He was almost gone with tuberculosis yet was unwilling to see any minister or religious person.

"Do please go with me now to see my son Harvey," she implored. "Maybe he'll listen to you."

I went to her house and found the young man too weak to talk much. Taking his emaciated hand, I said, "I see you are very low and weak. I do not wish to worry you with talking, but, from your appearance, I would judge that you have little hope of being restored to health."

He turned his head on his pillow as he said, "I can never be any better. I can't live."

"Then," I said, "your mind has been turned toward the future. May the enlightening influence of the Holy Spirit lead you to the Great Physician of souls, who knows every desire of the heart and is able to save to the uttermost—even at the eleventh hour."

Still holding his feverish hand in mine, I saw the starting tear as he looked earnestly at me.

I asked, "Will it be too much for you, in your weak condition, if I should read a few of the words of our Lord and Savior?"

"Oh no, I'd like to hear you."

I opened to the fourteenth chapter of John, and, after reading a few verses, I saw that the impression made was deepening. I asked if it would weary him too much if I should spend a few moments in prayer.

"Oh no, I'd like to hear you pray," he answered.

Placing my hand on his forehead, I implored divine aid in leading this precious soul to the cleansing fountain. I asked that his faith might increase and that, in its exercise, he be enabled to find the *"pearl of great price"* (Matthew 13:46).

As I arose from his bedside, he reached out both hands for mine and said, "I want you to come tomorrow." He wept freely; and I left with the burden of that precious soul upon my heart. The mother and sister, who were both Christians, stood near the door weeping for joy over the consent of their dear son and brother to listen to the reading and prayer.

The following day, I returned, and as soon as I entered, his mother said, "Oh, how thankful to God we are for this visit to my poor boy! He seems in almost constant prayer for mercy. Early this morning he spoke of your coming today."

As I entered his room, he threw up both hands, saying, "God will have mercy on poor me, won't He?"

"Most certainly," I responded. "His Word is *nigh* thee, even in thy heart and in thy mouth."

"Do pray for me," he requested.

I read a few words from the Bible and followed with prayer, in which he joined with a few interjections. I left him much more hopeful than on the previous day.

The next morning, his sister came for me in great haste, saying, "Brother Harvey wants to see you. Quick!"

It was not yet sunrise, but I hastened to obey the message, as I supposed he was dying. But, upon our opening the door, he exclaimed, "Glory to God, Mrs.

Haviland! Come to me quickly; I want to kiss you, for God brought me out of darkness this morning about the break of day! Oh, hallelujah! He shed His blood for poor me! Oh, how I wish I had strength to tell everybody that I am happier in one minute than I ever was in all my life put together."

He became quite exhausted, shouting and talking, and I advised him to rest now in the arms of the beloved Savior.

He answered, "Yes, I am in His arms."

About two hours before Harvey died, he looked at his mother, smiling, and said, "There's Mary! Don't you see her standing at the foot of my bed?"

"No, my son, Mother doesn't see her."

"Beautiful, beautiful she is. There, she's gone again."

Then, just as the soul took its flight, he raised both hands with a smile and said, "Here she is, with two angels with her. They've come for me."

The hands dropped as the breath left him, but the smile remained on his countenance.

The sister, Mary, had died a number of years previously at about the age of four. His mother told me that she had not heard her name mentioned in the family for months.

—Shaw, *Dying Testimonies of Saved and Unsaved*

# The Awful Death of William Pope

The following is a short account of the life and death of William Pope of Bolton, in Lancashire. He was, at one time, a member of the Methodist Church, and he seemed to be a saved and happy man. His wife, a devoted saint, died triumphantly. After her death, however, Pope's zeal for religion declined, and, by associating with backslidden hypocrites, he entered the path of ruin. His companions even professed to believe in the redemption of devils. William became an admirer of their scheme, a frequenter with them of the public house, and, in time, a common drunkard.

He finally became a disciple of Thomas Paine and associated himself with a number of deistical persons at Bolton. They would assemble together on Sundays to confirm each other in their infidelity and often amused themselves by throwing the Word of God on the floor, kicking it around the room, and treading it under their feet.

But, one day, God laid His hand on William Pope, and he was seized with tuberculosis. Mr. Rhodes was requested to visit him. He said, "When I first saw him, he said to me, 'Last night, I believe I was in hell and felt the horrors and torment of the damned, but God has brought me back again and given me a little longer respite. The gloom of guilty terror does not sit so heavy upon me as it did, and I have something like a faint hope that, after all I have done, God may yet save me.'

"After exhorting him to repentance and confidence in the almighty Savior, I prayed with him and left him. In the evening, he sent for me again. I found him in the utmost distress, overwhelmed with bitter anguish and despair. I endeavored to encourage him. I spoke of the infinite merit of the great Redeemer and mentioned several cases in which God had saved the greatest of sinners, but he answered, 'No case of any that has been mentioned is comparable to mine. I have no contrition; I cannot repent. God will damn me! I know the day of grace is lost. God has said of such as are in my case, "I will laugh at your calamity, and mock when your fear cometh."'

"I asked him if he had ever really known anything of the mercy and love of God. 'O yes,' he replied. 'Many years ago, I truly repented and sought the Lord and found peace and happiness.' I prayed with him and had great hopes of his salvation; he appeared much affected and begged I would represent his case in our church prayer meetings. I did so that evening, and many hearty petitions were put up for him."

Mr. Barraclough gave the following account of what he witnessed. He said, "I went to see William Pope, and, as soon as he saw me, he exclaimed, 'You are come to see one who is damned forever!' I answered, 'I hope not; Christ can save the chief of sinners.' He replied, 'I have denied Him; therefore He has cast me off forever! I know the day of grace is past, gone—gone, never more to return!' I entreated him not to be too hasty and to pray. He answered, 'I cannot pray; my heart is quite hardened. I have no desire to receive any blessing at the hand of God.' Then, he cried, 'O, the hell, the torment, the fire that I feel within me! O, eternity! Eternity! To dwell forever with devils and damned spirits in the burning lake must be my portion—and justly so!'

"On Thursday, I found him groaning under the weight of the displeasure of God. His eyes rolled to and fro; he lifted his hands and, with vehemence, cried out, 'O, the burning flame, the hell, the pain I feel! I have done the deed—the horrible, damnable deed!'

"I prayed with him, and, while I was praying, he said, with inexpressible rage, 'I will not have salvation at the hand of God! No. No! I will not ask it of Him!' After a short pause, he cried out, 'O, how I long to be in the bottomless pit—in the lake, which burns with fire and brimstone!'

"The day following, I saw him again. I said, 'William, your pain is inexpressible.' He groaned and, with a loud voice, cried out, 'Eternity will explain my torments. I tell you again, I am damned. I will not have salvation.'

"He called me to him as if to speak to me, but as soon as I came within his reach, he struck me on the head with all his might. Then, gnashing his teeth, he cried out, 'God will not hear your prayers!'

"At another time, he said, 'I have crucified the Son of God afresh and counted the blood of the covenant an unholy thing! O, that wicked and horrible deed of blaspheming against the Holy Spirit, which I know I have committed!' He was often heard to exclaim, 'I want nothing but hell! Come, O devil, and take me!'

"Another time, he said, 'O, what a terrible thing it is! Once I could, and would not; now I want and cannot!' He declared that he was best satisfied when cursing.

"The day he died, when Mr. Rhodes visited him and asked the privilege to pray once more with him, he cried out with great strength, considering his weakness, 'No!'

"That evening, he passed away—without God."

> There is a line by us unseen,
> That crosses every path,
> The hidden boundary between
> God's patience and His wrath.[13]

—Shaw, *Dying Testimonies of Saved and Unsaved*

13. J. A. Alexander, "There Is a Line by Us Unseen," 1900.

# Little Springett Penn
# (1696)

*The Second Son of William Penn, Founder of Pennsylvania*

All is mercy to me, dear Father—all is mercy to me. Though I cannot go to meeting, yet I have good meetings. The Lord comes in upon my spirit. I have heavenly meetings with Him by myself."

—Gottschall, *Selections from Testimonies and Dying Words*

# Beulah Blackman

*As told by Mrs. Anna M. Leonard of Manton, Michigan*

Beulah Blackman was a girl of unusual loveliness and strength of character. As a schoolteacher, she held up the light of a pure and holy life, often bringing persecution on herself by her unyielding adherence to the principles of Christianity and righteousness. On one occasion, while under the pressure of severe criticism, tears were streaming down her face as, with a smile, she told me, "This is good for me!"

She and my son, Lewis, were married in the summer of 1897. On Easter Sunday of the following year—the resurrection day—her spirit took its flight to be forever with the Lord. For months before she died, she was unable to go to church services, but she had her own "Bethel (house of God) experiences." Her little red Bible was always near, and the young girls who helped with her housework received advice and admonitions, which they will remember forever.

We were called to her home on Saturday evening, and when we entered the room, she held up her hands for loving greeting, saying, "Oh, Ma, the Lord is here, and I have the victory!" The Spirit came upon her, and she laughed and cried as we praised God together.

Upon the arrival of the doctor, she told him that a greater Physician than he had been there and had encouraged her so much. Since he was not a Christian, she added, "You don't understand it." All through that long night, she manifested such patient endurance. As her strength failed, she said, "I am so glad I have the Lord."

Just as the morning broke, bright and beautiful, she welcomed her infant son into the world with only time for one long kiss, and then to leave him motherless. Her heart, naturally weak, failed, and she appeared paralyzed. An effort was made to arouse her so that she could look again at her baby, but she could neither move nor speak. Her husband begged her to speak once more, but there was no answer. Then he asked her to smile if she still knew him. She did, and as he kissed her dear pale lips, they parted in an effort to return the demonstration of love.

After that, like a weary child going to sleep in its mother's arms, she leaned her head on Jesus' breast and breathed her life out sweetly there.

As we wept, she lifted her eyes upward and gazed an instant, as if surprised; then, a smile illuminated her face. A holy influence filled the room. There seemed to be angelic visitors waiting to conduct her home. The terror of death had fled, and our tears were dried. It seemed as if the gates of heaven were ajar, and a glimpse was given of the glory that awaits the faithful.

A moment more, and all was over. A look of peaceful victory rested on the lovely features. Truly God is our Father. He is love.

—Shaw, *Dying Testimonies of Saved and Unsaved*

# Sir Thomas Scott (1821)

Sir Thomas Scott was Privy Councillor of James V, King of Scotland, and a noted persecutor of the reformers. When dying, he cried out to the priests who sought to comfort him, "Begone, you and your trumpery; until this moment, I believed that there was neither a God nor a hell. Now, I know and feel that there are both, and I am doomed to perdition by just judgment."

—Gottschall, *Selections from Testimonies and Dying Words*

# William Foster (1887)

*As told by Mrs. Dorcas Eskridge of Blue Grove, Texas*

My father, William Foster, died April 2, 1887, near Chico, Texas, at the age of seventy-one. He was one of the purest Christians I had ever known and was often made happy in the Savior's love. He died praising God. His last words were, "My heaven! Heaven! Glory!"

I had often heard him remark that he did not believe Christians ever saw departed spirits while dying. I believed they did, so, to satisfy myself, I made a request during his sickness that if he came to die and should see spirits near him, he would tell me. If he wasn't able to speak, I told him to raise his hand in token that he saw them. Sure enough, just before consciousness left him, he raised his right hand and pointed upward.

I do praise the Lord for the dying testimony of one in whom I had so much confidence. Dear precious one! My mother also went home with the praise of God on her lips.

—Shaw, *Dying Testimonies of Saved and Unsaved*

# Catherine Seeley (1838)

It has been eleven years since I opened my eyes to the full light of day or borne my weight on my feet. But my darkened room has been cheered by the smiles of Jesus, the Son of Righteousness, whose blessed countenance sheds a luster upon everything that surrounds me and causes gratitude and praise to fill my soul. Death has no terrors!"

—Gottschall, *Selections from Testimonies and Dying Words*

# Frances Ridley Havergal (1879)

*English Poet and Hymn Writer*

This holy woman of God was born December 14, 1836, at Astley, England. She was the youngest daughter of Rev. William H. and Jane Havergal, her father being a distinguished minister of the Episcopal Church. She bore the name of Ridley in memory of the godly and learned Bishop Ridley, one of the noble army of martyrs. Many have been greatly helped by Miss Havergal's writings in both prose and verse.

She died June 3, 1879, at Caswell Bay, England. A short time before her death, she said to her sister Ellen, "I should have liked my death to be like Samson's, doing more for God's glory than by my life. But He wills it otherwise."

Ellen replied, "St. Paul said, 'The will of the Lord be done,' and 'Let Christ be magnified, whether by my life or by my death.'"

I think it was then that my beloved sister whispered, "Let my own text, 'The blood of Jesus Christ, His Son, cleanseth us from all sin,' be on my tomb. All the verse, if there is room."

She said to her sister, "I do not know what God means by it, but no new thoughts for poems or books come to me now." Later, she said, "In spite of the breakers, Marie, I am so happy God's promises are so true. Not a fear!"

When the doctor bid her good-bye and told her that he thought she was going, she answered, "Beautiful, too good to be true! Splendid to be so near the gate of heaven! So beautiful to go!"

The Vicar of Swansea said to her, "You have talked and written a good deal about the King, and you will soon see Him in His beauty. Is Jesus with you now?"

"Of course," she replied. "It is splendid! I thought He would have left me here a long while, but He is so good to take me now."

At another time, she said, "Oh, I want all of you to speak bright, bright words about Jesus. Oh, do, do! It is all perfect peace. I am only waiting for Jesus to take me in."

Then, later, she sang the following stanza:

> Jesus, I will trust Thee,
> Trust Thee with my soul;
> Guilty, lost, and helpless,
> Thou canst make me whole.
> There is none in heaven
> Or on earth like Thee:
> Thou hast died for sinners—
> Therefore Lord for me.[14]

With deep feeling, she emphasized that last word, "me."

There came a terrible rush of convulsive sickness; it ceased, the nurse gently assisting her. She nestled down in the pillows and folded her hands on her breast, saying, "There, now it's all over. Blessed rest!"

Then, all at once, she looked up steadfastly, as if she saw the Lord—and, surely, nothing less heavenly could have reflected such a glorious radiance upon her face. For ten minutes, we watched that almost visible meeting with her King.

14. Mary J. Walker, "Jesus, I Will Trust Thee," 1855.

Her countenance was so glad, as if she were already talking to Him.

She tried to sing, but after one sweet, high note, "He...," her voice failed. As her brother commended her soul into her Redeemer's hand, she passed away. Our precious sister was gone—satisfied, glorified, within the palace of her King!

—Shaw, *Dying Testimonies of Saved and Unsaved*

# Girolamo Savonarola (1498)

*The Great Italian Reformer*

When the bishop announced the words "I separate thee from the church," a sudden hope lit up the martyr's face, and he exclaimed, "From the church militant, but not from the church triumphant! My Lord died for my sins; shall not I gladly give my life for Him?"

—Gottschall, *Selections from Testimonies and Dying Words*

# Thomas Hobbes (1679)

Thomas Hobbes was born April 5, 1588, at Malmesbury, in Wiltshire, England, and died December 4, 1679, at Hardwick Hall, in Devonshire. He was educated at Magdalen Hall, Oxford, and, during the first part of his life, up to 1637, he worked as a tutor in various noble families, often traveling on "the Continent" with his pupils. The remainder of his life was spent in a comprehensive, vigorous literary activity, first in Paris, then in London, or in the country with the

Hardwick family. The philosophical standpoint of Hobbes may be described as an application to the study of man and of the method and principles of the study of nature. The results of this process were a psychology and a code of morals utterly antagonistic not only to Christianity, but to religion in general.

When the atheist Hobbes drew near to death, he declared, "I am about to take a leap in the dark!" The last sensible words he uttered were, "I shall be glad to find a hole to creep out of the world."

—Shaw, *Dying Testimonies of Saved and Unsaved*

# Sir Thomas Smith (1577)

*Secretary of State to Queen Elizabeth*

It is a matter of lamentation that men know not for what end they were born into the world until they are ready to go out of it."

—Gottschall, *Selections from Testimonies and Dying Words*

# An Infidel's Life Spared a Few Days

During the summer of 1862, I became acquainted with a Mr. A—, who professed infidelity, and who was, I think, as near an atheist as anyone I've ever met. I had several conversations with him but could not seem to make any impression on his mind, for whenever I pressed a point strongly, he would become angry.

In the fall, he was taken ill and seemed to go into a rapid decline. I, with others, sought kindly and prayerfully to turn his mind to his need of a Savior, but we only met with rebuffs. However, as I saw the end drawing near, one day, I pressed the importance of preparing to meet God. He became angry and said I need not trouble myself anymore about his soul, as there was no God, the Bible was a fable, and, when we die, that is the last of us. He was unwilling that I should pray with him, so I left him, feeling very sad.

Some four weeks later, on New Year's morning, I awoke with the distinct impression that I should go see Mr. A—. I could not get rid of the impression, so, about nine o'clock, I went to see him.

As I approached the house, I saw two doctors leaving. I rang the bell, and when his sister-in-law opened the door for me, she exclaimed, "Oh! I am so glad you have come. John is dying! The doctors say he cannot possibly live more than two hours, and probably not one."

I went to his room and found him bolstered upright in a chair. He appeared to have fallen asleep. I sat down about five feet from him, and, in about two minutes, he opened his eyes and saw me. There was agony on his face and in the tone of his voice as he exclaimed, "Oh, I am not prepared to die! There *is* a God; the Bible *is* true! Oh, pray for me! Pray God to spare me a few days till I shall know I am saved!"

These words were uttered with the most intense emotion, while his whole physical frame quivered from the intense agony of his soul. I replied, in effect, that Jesus was a great Savior, able and willing to save all who would come unto Him, even at the eleventh hour, as He did the thief on the cross.

When I was about to pray with him, he again entreated me to pray especially that God would spare him a few days, till he might have the evidences of his salvation. In prayer, I seemed to have great assurance of his salvation, and I asked God to give us the evidence of his salvation by granting him a few more days in this world. Several others joined in praying God to spare him in this way.

I called again in the evening. He seemed stronger than in the morning, and his mind was seeking the truth. The next day, as I entered, his face expressed the fact that peace and joy had taken the place of fear and anxiety.

He was spared some five days, giving very clear evidence that he had passed from death to life. His case was a great mystery to the doctors. They could not understand how he lived so long, but we who had been praying for him all knew it was in direct answer to prayer.

—Shaw, *Dying Testimonies of Saved and Unsaved*

# St. Stephen
## (c. 34)

*Stoned to Death as the First Christian Martyr*

*Behold, I see the heavens opened, and the Son of man standing on the right hand of God. Then they cried out with a loud voice, and stopped their ears, and ran upon him with one accord, and cast him out of the city, and stoned him: and the witnesses laid down their clothes at a young man's feet, whose name was Saul. And they stoned Stephen, calling upon God, and saying, Lord Jesus, receive my spirit....Lord, lay not this sin to their charge"* (Acts 7:56–60).

# Gertrude Belle Butterfield
## (1898)

*As told by Cora A. Niles*

My beloved friend, Gertrude Belle Butterfield, spent her last day on earth on May 24, 1898, when she passed on to that fairer country whose inhabitants count not the days nor the years. Only twenty-four years of the earthly life were given her.

In early adolescence, she learned the beauty of a life in God's service and became willing to spend and be spent for Him. Part of her service was evangelistic work, and only the last great garnering time will tell how many soul-sheaves ripened from seeds of her sowing. When she saw the field of labor widening, she consecrated her life to mission work in foreign lands, should God lead the way.

Upon graduating from the Evansville Seminary, a little less than a year before her death, she returned to her home near Reedsburg, Wisconsin. She was weary and worn from work and study but thought rest was all that was needful. She felt that life was before her and that she was just ready to live. Love from one worthy—life's richest gift—had come to her, and her heart was satisfied.

But it was not long ere she knew that the weariness was tuberculosis and that life's plans must be put aside. In a letter written in January, she said, "Oh, it would be easy to go, so easy, if it were not for my life work all undone. I cannot but feel that it would please Him to let me live and work for souls who know not my Jesus." Later, however, even that unfinished work was given up to Him, and all was at rest. Dreams of heaven came to her, and she was ready, yes, glad to go.

The last months of her life were full of suffering, but there was no complaint. "Everyone is so kind" often fell from her lips at some attention from those who tenderly ministered to her wants.

Very precious is the memory of some days spent with her three weeks before her death. She was so pure, so gentle, so thoughtful of others—so like Him who had put upon her *"the beauty of the Lord"* (Psalm 27:4).

As the end approached, her sufferings became intense. The Sunday evening before she went home, all thought the death angel very near. She asked her friends to sing the beautiful hymn…

> Fade, fade, each earthly joy,
> Jesus is mine!
> Break every tender tie,
> Jesus is mine!
> Dark is the wilderness, earth has no resting place,
> Jesus alone can bless, Jesus is mine![15]

For days, she had scarcely spoken above a whisper, but now, the Spirit of the Lord came upon her in blessing, and as she raised her hands, she repeated, in a voice clear and strong, "*'O death, where is thy sting? O grave, where is thy victory?*'" (1 Corinthians 15:55). "*'Yea, though I walk through the valley of the shadow of death, I will fear no evil: for thou art with me; thy rod and thy staff they comfort me*'" (Psalm 23:4).

15. Jane C. Bonar, "Jesus Is Mine," 1843.

She was so eager for the release, asking those near her if they thought it the last, and saying, "Oh, I hope I won't be disappointed."

But not until Tuesday afternoon did the end come and the soul escape as a bird from its prison of pain. And we who await this dawning light that so thrilled her soul treasure the memory of one "*faithful unto death*" (Revelation 2:10), our sainted Gertrude.

—Shaw, *Dying Testimonies of Saved and Unsaved*

# Isaac Shoemaker (1779)

O that I could tell you what I have seen and undergone! It would pierce the hardest heart among you. Perhaps some may think there is no hell, but I have to tell you that there is a hell, and a dreadful one, too. And there is a heaven where angels clothed in white robes sit at the right hand of God, singing praises to His great name."

—Gottschall, *Selections from Testimonies and Dying Words*

# "You Gave Me Nothing to Hold On *To*"

In a Pennsylvania country village, a physician gave books on infidelity to a young man and persuaded him to deny his Savior.

Later in life, in 1875, when the young man was fifty years of age, he died. The infidel teacher was his physician, and, as the end was approaching, he urged the dying man to die as he had lived—as a "rejector" of God and Christ.

"Hold on to the end," urged the doctor.

"Yes, doctor," said the dying man, "there is just my trouble—you gave me nothing to hold on *to*."

The doctor did not reply.

—Shaw, *Dying Testimonies of Saved and Unsaved*

# "Look at the Little Children! Oh, Ma, I Must Go!"

*As told by Mrs. T. W. Roberts of East Nashville, Tennessee*

My little sister, Minnie Chatham, died in 1873 at the age of twelve.

She was always of a sweet, gentle, and religious nature, and she dearly loved Sunday school and her teachers. Her constant prayer was, "O God, give me a new heart." Sometimes her older friends would say, "Why, Minnie, you are a good little girl; you don't need to pray for a new heart." But she would reply, "Yes, I do. There is none good; we are all sinners."

During her sickness, which lasted two weeks, she suffered greatly, and Father and Mother stayed with her constantly, night and day. One day, she managed to get out of bed and kneel at the footboard. With her hands clasped and eyes lifted toward heaven, she prayed the most earnest prayer that I have ever heard. She prayed, "O Lord, give me a new heart," after which she spoke the Lord's Prayer. She then arose, clapped her hands, and said, "Oh, I am so happy!" Returning to her bed, she lay down and was as peaceful and quiet as if she had never experienced any pain.

Her mother had told her that Jesus could ease her pain; therefore, often, when she was suffering, we saw her little hands clasped in prayer. Sometimes she would sing a verse or two of her Sunday school songs that she loved so well. She called for her Testament and Sunday school papers, which she placed under her pillow and kept there until she died.

Shortly before she breathed her last, she sat up in bed and said, "The angels have come for me; I must go! They are at the door waiting for me. Do, Ma, let me go! Why do you want to keep me here in this wicked world? I would not want to stay here for anything." And then, she looked up toward heaven and continued, "Look at the little children! Oh, Ma, I must go! I would not want to do anything to displease my dear Savior."

After this, she called her father to her bedside, requested him to be good and meet her in heaven, and then added, "I want you all to be good."

The next morning, she said to her mother, "Now, Ma, if you had let me go, I would have been with the angels this morning."

The day before she died, she sang her favorite Sunday school song:

> There is no name so sweet on earth,
> No name so sweet in heaven,
> The name, before His wondrous birth,
> To Christ the Savior given.
>
> We love to sing of Christ our King,
> And hail Him, blessed Jesus,
> For there's no word ear ever heard
> So dear, so sweet as "Jesus."[16]

Not long after this, she closed her eyes and breathed her last, as peacefully as if she had just fallen asleep.

Her public school teacher came to see her the day after she died. As she gazed at the little silent face in the coffin, she wept as though her heart would break. She said Minnie was the brightest and sweetest child she had ever met and was a perfect example for all her classes.

—Shaw, *Dying Testimonies of Saved and Unsaved*

16. George W. Bethune, "There Is No Name So Sweet on Earth," 1858.

# Margaret Wilson (1685)

During the reign of Charles II, Margaret Wilson, a girl of eighteen, was condemned to be drowned as a Protestant, along with a widow of sixty-three.

Two stakes were driven deep into the sand, but the one for the widow was placed further down the beach. The persecutors hoped that the young girl's fortitude might be shaken by watching the older woman's sufferings.

The tide rose, and the widow struggled in her drowning agony. A heartless ruffian asked Margaret, "What do you think of your friend now?"

The undaunted young martyr answered, "What do I see but Christ in one of His members wrestling there? Think you that we are the sufferers? No, it is Christ in us! He does not send us to warfare at our own charges."

—Gottschall, *Selections from Testimonies and Dying Words*

# Jerome of Prague (1416)

This great Bohemian reformer suffered martyrdom at the stake May 30, 1416, in Constance, the same place where his friend and mentor, the priest John Hus, was burned.

On arriving at the place of execution, Jerome embraced the stake with great cheerfulness, and when the fagots were set on fire behind him, he said, "Come here and kindle it before my eyes, for if I had been afraid of it, I would not have come to this place."

We take the following from *The Schaff-Herzog Encyclopedia of Religious Knowledge* (1805):

> Jerome studied at Oxford, probably in 1396, and returned to Prague with Wycliffe's theological writings. In 1398, he took the degree of bachelor of arts at Prague and, subsequently, that of master in Paris. Upon his return to Prague in 1407, he entered into hearty sympathy with the plans of Hus. In 1410, he went, on the invitation of the king of Poland, to assist in putting the University of Cracow on a secure basis, and, from there, he traveled to preach before Sigismund, king of Hungary. Being suspected of heretical doctrines, however, he fled to Vienna but was put in prison, from which he was only released on the requisition of the University of Prague.
>
> When, in October 1414, Hus was about to leave for Constance, Jerome encouraged him to fortitude and promised to go to his assistance if necessary. On April 4, 1415, he fulfilled his promise but, on the advice of the Bohemian nobles, fled from Constance the day after his arrival. He was recognized at Hirschau by his denunciations of the council, taken prisoner, and sent back to Constance in chains.
>
> After Hus' death, the council attempted to induce Jerome to retract and succeeded on September tenth. However, the day following, he withdrew his retraction. The council instituted a second trial, but not until the following May (1416) was he granted a public hearing. All attempts to move him again were unavailing. On May 30, he was condemned by the council as a heretic.
>
> As the flames crept about him, he sang the Easter hymn "Hail, Festal Day" and repeated the three articles of the Apostolic Creed concerning God the Father, Son, and Holy Ghost.
>
> The last words he was heard to say were, "This soul in flames I offer, Christ, to Thee!"

—Shaw, *Dying Testimonies of Saved and Unsaved*

# A Dying Mother Warns Her Children

*As told by Dr. L. B. Balliett of Allentown, Pennsylvania*

A mother, who denied Christ and sneered at religion, came to her dying bed. Looking up from her restless pillow at the group of weeping sons and daughters gathered at her bedside, she said, "My children, I have been leading you on the wrong road all of your lives. I now find that the broad road leads to destruction—I did not believe it before. Oh! Seek to serve God and to find the gate of heaven, though you may never meet your mother there."

So amidst clouds and darkness set the sun of her life.

—Shaw, *Dying Testimonies of Saved and Unsaved*

# Peace in the Storm

*As told by Dr. L. B. Balliett of Allentown, Pennsylvania*

Some years ago, a steamer was sinking with hundreds of persons onboard. Only one boatload was saved. As a man was leaping from the ship's side, a young girl who could not be taken into the boat handed him a note, saying, "Give this to my mother."

The man was saved, but the girl, like hundreds of others, drowned.

The mother eventually received the note. These were the words written on it:

"Dear mother, you must not grieve for me; I am going to Jesus."

—Shaw, *Dying Testimonies of Saved and Unsaved*

# Joseph Duncan (1844)

*Governor of Illinois*

Joseph Duncan was born in 1794 in Kentucky. After serving in the War of 1812, he moved to Illinois, where, as a member of the state senate, he originated a law establishing common schools. He was elected a member of Congress in 1827 and governor of Illinois in 1843. He died January 15, 1844. We take the following from *The Higher Christian Life* by Rev. William Edwin Boardman (1858):

> For many years the governor was distinguished as a Christian—a consistent member of his church. He was a rare and shining mark, both for the jests of ungodly politicians and for the happy references of all lovers of Jesus.
>
> It is a very lovely and remarkable thing to see one occupying the highest position of honor in a state, himself honoring the King of Kings. Happy is the people who exalt such a ruler to the places of power, and happy such a ruler in his exaltation—more, however, in the humility with which he bows to Jesus than in the homage which the people pay to him.
>
> His conversion was clear. He renounced all merit of his own as grounds for his acceptance with God. The blood of Jesus, the Lamb of Calvary, was all his hope. And all went well until death and the judgment drew near.
>
> About three weeks before the hour of his death, he was seized with the illness that he himself felt would end his life.
>
> With the premonition of death came the question of fitness for heaven. He became troubled. The fever of his mind was higher than the fever in his veins—and, alas, he had not yet learned that Jesus is the Physician of unfailing skill to cure every ill to which the spirit is heir.

He saw plainly enough how he could be justified from the law, that it should not condemn him; for its penalty had been borne already by the Savior Himself, and its claims on the score of justice were all satisfied. But he did not see that the same hands which had been nailed to the cross would also break off the manacles of sin, wash out its stains, and adjust the spotless robe of Christ's perfect righteousness upon him, investing him with every heavenly grace.

His perplexity was great. As the night thickened upon him, his soul was in agony, and his struggles utterly vain. The point of despair is sure to be reached, sooner or later, by the struggling soul, and the point of despair to him who abandons all to Jesus is also the point of hope.

The governor at last gave over and gave up, saying in his heart, "Ah! Well. I see it is of no use. Die I must. Fit myself for heaven I cannot. O, Lord Jesus, I must throw myself upon Thy mercy and die as I am."

This hopeless abandonment was the beginning of rest to his soul. Indeed, it was the victory that overcometh, and soon, the loveliness of Jesus began to be unfolded to him. He saw that the way of salvation from sin's power is just the same as with salvation from sin's guilt—through simple faith in the Savior.

The fire in his veins burned on, steadily and surely consuming the vital forces of his manly frame, but the fever of his spirit was all allayed by the copious and cooling draughts given him from the gushing fountain of the waters of life flowing from Jesus, the smitten Rock—and his joy was unbounded.

As his stricken and sorrowing family gathered around his bed for the last words of the noble man, he told them, with a face radiant with joy, that he had just found what was worth more to him than riches, or honors, or office, or anything else upon earth—the way of salvation by faith in the Lord Jesus Christ. He then charged them as his dying mandate, by the love they bore him, not to rest until they, too—whether already Christians, as he himself long had been, or not—had found the same blessed treasure.

They mentioned the name of a distinguished fellow officer and special friend of the governor's living in a distant part of the state and asked if he had any message for him.

"Tell him that I have found the way of salvation by faith in the Lord Jesus Christ, and, if he will also find it for himself, it will be better than the highest offices and honors in the reach of man upon earth."

So he died. "If he had only known this before," you say. Yes, that was just what he himself said: "Oh, had I only known this when I first engaged in the service of God, how happy I should have been! And how much good I could have done!"

—Shaw, *Dying Testimonies of Saved and Unsaved*

# Dr. Washington Manly Wingate (1879)

In his last moments, Dr. Wingate, longtime president of Wake Forest College in North Carolina, was heard personally talking to the Master as follows:

"Oh, how delightful it is! I knew You would be with me when the time came, and I knew it would be sweet—but not as sweet as it is!"

—Gottschall, *Selections from Testimonies and Dying Words*

# "I Am Going to Hell!"

A preacher in the West sends us the sad account of his grandfather's death. He says,

My grandfather spent three years on the plains with the noted Indian scout Kit Carson, but he always had been an unsaved man.

During the last three months of his life, when he was sick, he would often send for me to talk with him on the subject of religion. However, when pressed to seek the Lord at once, he would say, "I have got along so long, I think I will wait a while longer."

He died July 3, 1883, and almost (if not) the last words he uttered were these: "I am going to hell!"

Awfully sad, fearfully true, he put off the most important duty of this life until it was too late, forever too late.

—Shaw, *Dying Testimonies of Saved and Unsaved*

# Martin Luther (1546)

This great German reformer was born November 10, 1483, at Eisleben, a town in Saxony not far from Wittenberg. He died February 18, 1546, at the same place. We take the following from *The Schaff-Herzog Encyclopedia of Religious Knowledge* (1805):

Luther stands forth as the great national hero of the German people and the ideal of German life. Perhaps no other cultivated nation has a hero who so completely expresses the national ideal. King Arthur comes, perhaps, nearest to Luther among the English-speaking race.

He was great in his private life as well as in his public career. His home was the ideal of cheerfulness and song. He was great in thought and great in action. He was a severe student, yet skilled in the knowledge of men. He was humble in the recollection of the power and designs of a personal Satan, yet bold and defiant in the midst of all perils. He could beard the papacy and imperial councils, yet he fell trustingly before the cross. He was never weary, and there seemed to be no limit to his creative energy.

Thus, Luther stands before the German people as the type of German character. Goethe, Frederick the Great, and all others, in this regard, pale before the German reformer. He embodies, in his single person, the boldness of the battlefield, the song of the musician, the joy and care of the parent, the skill of the writer, the force of the orator, and the sincerity of rugged manhood—but also the humility of the Christian.

His last words were, "O my heavenly Father, my eternal and everlasting God! Thou hast revealed to me Thy Son, our Lord Jesus Christ! I have preached Him! I have confessed Him! I love Him and I worship Him as my dearest Savior and Redeemer! Into Thy hands I commit my spirit."

—Shaw, *Dying Testimonies of Saved and Unsaved*

# John Wilmot (1680)

*Second Earl of Rochester*

John Wilmot was saved from a life of deep sin and infidelity. When dying, he laid his hand upon the Bible and said, in earnestness and solemnity,

> The only objection against this Book is a bad life; I shall die now, but, oh, what unspeakable glories do I see! What joys beyond thought or expression am I sensible of! I am assured of God's mercy to me through Jesus Christ. Oh, how I long to die!

—Gottschall, *Selections from Testimonies and Dying Words*

# Dying in Despair

About 1880, while we were doing some evangelistic work early one morning, a little boy with a sad heart called at our room to say that his mother was dying and wished to see us. We hurried to his home, and as we opened the door, we beheld a sorrowful sight: a woman in complete despair. The expression on her face and the sad look in her eyes told of great agony.

We were at a loss to know just what to say or do. Our heart was full. We said to her, "You are in great pain."

With a wild look, she replied, "Yes, I am in great pain; but that is nothing compared with the thought of going to meet God unprepared. What is this physical suffering compared to the remorse of conscience and the dark future before me!"

Then, she cried out in agony, "All is vanity! I have lived for self and tried to find pleasure at the dance and other places of amusement. I have neglected the salvation of my soul! I am unprepared to meet God! Pray for me, oh, pray for me!"

While we prayed, she would say, "God help me! What shall I do? Is there any hope for a poor sinner like me?" Her ungodly husband cried bitterly as she told of their past sinful lives. Her heart was hardened with sin; her ears were dull of hearing; her eyes too blind to see the light of God.

Her friends were coming from the village and surrounding countryside to see her die. As they entered the room, she would take each one of them by the hand and plead with them not to follow her example and live as she had lived. Holding an uncle by the hand, a man deep in sin who seemed to be far from God, she said, "Uncle, prepare to meet your God. Don't wait until you come to your dying day, as I have done. When you plow your ground, pray. When you plant your corn, pray. When you cultivate, pray. Whatever you do, pray!"

Many of her friends wept and promised to live better lives. Her mental agony was so far beyond her physical pain that she seemed to be unconscious of her intense bodily suffering. Her sins seemed to loom up before her as a great mountain, hiding from her the presence and love of God.

As long as she was able to speak, she prayed and requested others to do so, but, finally, the voice that had been pleading so pitifully for mercy and warning others by the example of her ungodly life was hushed in the silence of death.

Soon after her death, we called on her husband and reminded him of his wife's dying testimony, urging him to attend the evangelistic meetings we were holding in the town. But he was full of prejudice against Christianity and gave us no encouragement. He continued to walk in the same sinful path as before.

—Shaw, *Dying Testimonies of Saved and Unsaved*

# "I Am So Glad That I Have Always Loved Jesus"

*Adapted from a letter by Mollie J. Herring of Clear Run, North Carolina*

Miss Orphie B. Schaeffer, daughter of Rev. G. F. Schaeffer, a Lutheran minister, who, at that time, was president of the North Carolina Lutheran College, was visiting at our home, and we soon became very warm friends. Suddenly, however, Orphie was taken ill, her sickness developing into a serious case of typhus fever, which resulted in her death two weeks later.

During her illness, she would often speak of her loved ones far away in Easton, Pennsylvania. We had not wired them of her illness, as we did not realize that it was of such a serious nature until the end drew near.

She loved her Savior and put her utmost confidence in God. Often, she would say, "It is so sweet to love Jesus. I have always loved Him."

As I stood at her bedside as she was dying, she called me to come closer to her and said, "Mollie, I hear the sweetest music." I asked her where the sound of the music came from, and she replied, "Oh, just over the hill. Do you not hear them say, 'Peace on earth, goodwill toward men'?"

Again, her wan features lighted up with the very light of heaven, and she said, "Oh, can't you hear them singing? Do listen."

I strained my eager ears to catch the sound to which I knew she was listening, but I could hear nothing, save for her labored breathing.

Soon afterward, she said, "Good-bye, Mama! Good-bye, Florence! Good-bye, Papa!" Then she was seized with a hemorrhage that caused her to grow weaker and weaker.

Finally, just before the last, we heard her say once more, "I am so glad that I have always loved Jesus."

—Shaw, *Dying Testimonies of Saved and Unsaved*

# Chief Vara

*A Warrior*

In the days of his ignorance, Chief Vara had been a mighty Patagonian warrior who had offered human sacrifices. After his conversion, however, he became a devoted Christian.

"I have been very wicked, but a great king from the other side of the skies sent his ambassadors with terms of peace. We could not tell for many years what these ambassadors wanted, but, at length, King Pomare invited all his subjects to come and take refuge under the wings of Jesus. I was one of the first to do so.

"The blood of Jesus is my foundation, and I grieve that all my children do not know Him. My outside man and my inside man differ. Let the one rot till the trumpet shall sound, but let my soul wing her way to Jesus!"

—Gottschall, *Selections from Testimonies and Dying Words*

# "Murder! Murder! Murder!"

*Adapted from an article in* California Life Illustrated

When Mr. R—, from Baltimore, was seized with cholera, he sent for me. When I entered the room, he said, "My wife, who is a Christian woman, has been writing to me ever since I came here, urging me to make your acquaintance and attend your church. But I have not done it, and, what is worse, I am about to leave the world with no preparation to meet God."

He was a noble-looking man, and since I knew many of his friends in Baltimore, I felt the greatest possible sympathy for him. My soul loved him, and

I determined, if possible, to contest the devil's claim on him to the last moment of his life.

But he was in despair, and, after I had labored with him about an hour, urging him to try to fix his mind on some precious promise of the Bible, he said, "There is but one passage in the Bible that I can call to mind, and that haunts me. I can think of nothing else; it exactly suits my case: '*He, that being often reproved hardeneth his neck, shall suddenly be destroyed, and that without remedy*' (Proverbs 29:1).

"Mr. Taylor," he continued, "it's no use to talk to me or to try to do anything further. I am *that* man, and my doom is fixed."

The next day, when I entered his room, he said to a couple of young men present, "Go out, boys; I want to talk to Mr. Taylor." Then, he said, "I have no hope, but for the warning of others, I want to tell you something that occurred a few months ago, when I was in health and doing a good business. A man said to me, 'Dick, how would you like to have a clerkship?' I replied, 'I wouldn't have a clerkship, even under Jesus Christ.' Now, sir, that is an example of the way I treated Christ when I thought I did not need Him. Now, when I'm dying and can do no better in this life, it's presumption to offer myself to Him. It is no use; He won't have me."

Nothing that I could say seemed to have any effect toward changing his mind.

A few hours afterward, when he felt the icy grasp of death upon his heart, he cried, "Boys, help me out of this place!"

"No, Dick, you're too sick," they replied. "We cannot help you to get up."

"Oh, do help me up! I can't lie here!"

"Please, Dick, don't exert yourself so; you'll hasten your death."

"Boys!" gasped the poor fellow. "If you don't help me up, I'll cry 'Murder!'" And with that, he cried at the top of his voice, "Murder! Murder! Murder!" till life's tide ebbed out and his voice was hushed in death.

How dreadful the hazard of postponing the great object for which life is given to the hour when heart and flesh are failing!

—Shaw, *Dying Testimonies of Saved and Unsaved*

# Bishop John Jacob Glossbrenner (1887)

"*Say ye to the righteous, that it shall be well with him*" (Isaiah 3:10). So it was with the devout Bishop Glossbrenner when he had reached the end of his earthly pilgrimage on January 7, 1887.

Mr. John Dodds of Dayton, Ohio, a personal friend of the bishop, spent a day or two with him shortly before his death and found him in a most blessed frame of mind. When the subject of preaching was referred to, the bishop said, "If I could preach again, just once more, I would preach Jesus. I would preach from His words to the disciples on the Sea of Galilee, '*It is I; be not afraid*' (Mark 6:50)."

As Mr. Dodds was leaving, he looked back, and, to his surprise, the bishop had gotten out of bed unassisted and was standing by the door. Visibly affected, and with hand uplifted and tears running down his cheeks, he said, "Tell my brethren it is all right. My home is over there!"

To another, he said, "My title is clear, but not because I have preached the gospel, but alone by the love and mercy and grace of our Lord Jesus Christ. Rely upon nothing but Jesus Christ and an experimental knowledge of acceptance with God through the merits of Jesus."

In view of his rapidly approaching end, he said to his pastor, "I shall not be here much longer." When asked about the future, he replied, "Everything is as bright as it can be. What a blessing it is to have a Savior at a time like this."

His last whispered words were, "My Savior!"

—Shaw, *Dying Testimonies of Saved and Unsaved*

# Hugh Latimer (1555)

*Martyr of the English Reformation*

Hugh Latimer, one of the most influential preachers, foremost leaders, and heroic martyrs of the English Reformation, was born around 1485 at Thurcaston, Leicestershire. Latimer had been appointed Bishop of Worcester in 1535 but was forced to resign his bishopric in 1539 when he opposed Henry VIII's Six Articles. Later, he became the Church of England chaplain to King Edward VI.

His Protestant beliefs led him to be tried and committed to the Tower of London as a "seditious fellow" in 1555, under the reign of the Catholic queen Mary I. To the Tower, his fellow Oxford martyrs, Nicholas Ridley and Thomas Cranmer, were also sent. In March of that year, all three had been brought before the queen's commissioners at Oxford, condemned for heresy, and sent back into confinement.

Seven months later, Latimer and Ridley were brought to Oxford to be burned at the stake. When stripped for execution, Latimer had on a long shroud. There he stood, this withered old man, perfectly happy, with a bag of powder tied around his neck. The two men embraced each other at the stake, knelt and prayed, and then kissed the stake.

Just as the fire was lighted, Latimer addressed his fellow sufferer with these memorable words: "Play the man, Master Ridley; we shall this day light such a candle, by God's grace, in England, as I trust shall never be put out!"

As the flames leaped up, Latimer cried, "O Father of heaven, receive my soul!"

He seemed to embrace the flames. Having stroked his face, he bathed his hands in the fire and quickly died.

To Roman Catholicism, that fire was the costliest ever kindled. To England—thank God—it was the light of religious liberty, the candle of the Reformation.

—John Vaughan, *Life Stories of Remarkable Preachers* (1892)

# Giles Tilleman (1544)

*A Martyr from Brussels*

Giles Tilleman, a cutler of Brussels, was a man of great humanity and piety. Among others, he was apprehended as a Protestant, and many endeavors were made by the monks to persuade him to recant. When an opportunity to escape prison offered itself, Tilleman would not take advantage of it, saying, "I would not do the keepers so much injury, as they would have to answer for my absence."

At the stake, the executioner offered to strangle him before the fire was lighted, but he would not consent, saying that he did not fear the flames. There was a large pile of wood at the place of execution. He asked that the principal part of it be given to the poor, saying, "A small quantity will suffice to consume me."

He then died with much composure.

—Gottschall, *Selections from Testimonies and Dying Words*

# Abandoned to Die Alone

*As told by Milburn Merrill of Denver, Colorado*

P— K— was a talented and wealthy man, but he hated everything connected with God, the Lord Jesus Christ, and the Holy Bible. He talked, lectured, and published books and tracts against the Savior and the sacred Scriptures, circulating them freely wherever he could. His influence for evil was very great for many years.

From a neighbor and members of his household, the following facts are learned concerning his death:

His deathbed beggared description. He clenched his teeth, and blood spurted from his nostrils, while he cried, "Hell! Hell!! Hell!" with a terror that no pen can describe. A neighbor declared that he had heard the screams a quarter of a mile away.

His family could not endure the agony of that deathbed scene. They fled to an adjoining wood across the road and there remained, among the trees, until all became quiet at home. One by one, they ventured back to find the husband and father cold in death. He literally had been left to die alone, abandoned of God and of man.

—Shaw, *Dying Testimonies of Saved and Unsaved*

# Rev. William Kendall (1858)

*Adapted from Sarah A. Cooke,* Wayside Sketches *(1896)*

Coworker with Dr. Redfield and the glorious little band of early Free Methodists was the Rev. William Kendall. He died February 1, 1858, and the closing scenes of his life were so blessed that we give them a place here:

He revived on the Sunday before his death and was very happy, his face radiant with glory. He said, "This is the most blessed Sunday I ever knew."

The next day, he had a severe conflict with Satan but gained a glorious victory. He said, "Jesus the mighty Conqueror reigns!"

The next day, he exclaimed, "Why, heaven has come down to earth! I see the angels. They are flying through the house!"

After a little sleep, he awoke and exclaimed, "I have seen the King in His beauty—King of glory. I have slept in His palace!"

For a while, he was delirious. Again, he had a conflict with the powers of darkness, but he quickly triumphed, exclaiming with a smile, "I can grapple with the grim monster, death."

On Sunday, he was thought to be dying. His wife put her ear to his lips as he lay gazing upward and waving his arms, as though fluttering to be gone. She heard him breathe, "Hail! All hail!"

"What do you see?" she asked.

"I see light! Light! Light! I see...." He paused in silence for a while, then suddenly began to sing in a clear, though somewhat faltering, tone,

> Hallelujah to the Lamb, who hath purchased our pardon!
> We will praise Him again when we pass over Jordan.[17]

One asked, "Is all well?"

He replied, with ineffable sweetness, "All is well! All is well! All is well!"

The chill of death came and pointed to his speedy relief, but once more he revived and sang very sweetly, "O how happy are they who their Savior obey."

Then, he followed with,

> My soul's full of glory, inspiring my tongue;
> Could I meet with the angels, I'd sing them a song.[18]

A few more struggles of nature and the silver cord loosened, and the warrior fell to rise immortal.

—Shaw, *Dying Testimonies of Saved and Unsaved*

# Peter the Great (1725)

*Czar of Russia*

Filled with remorse because of his cruelty toward his son, in his dying hour, Peter the Great cried, "I believe, Lord, and confess; help my unbelief!"

—Gottschall, *Selections from Testimonies and Dying Words*

17. Richard Birdsall, "The Voice of Free Grace Cries," 1820.
18. Unknown, "The Dying Christian."

# "I Can See the Angels All in the Room"

*Adapted from a letter by Mrs. Anna Crowson of China Spring, Texas, c. 1898*

My beloved mother's death was one of triumph and great victory. She was a woman of great faith who made the Bible her constant study. Some years before her death, realizing that she could be established in the faith, she went to God in earnest prayer and made an entire consecration. By faith, she was enabled to take Christ as a complete Savior, and she knew that the blood of Jesus cleansed her from all her sin. From that time, she lived in an ocean of God's love and was kept from all sin by the power of God through faith.

One Sunday morning, while preparing for church, Mother took a chill. From that time on, she knew she was going to die. She remarked to her eldest daughter, "I have been looking for something to happen for a long time to bring Father back to Jesus, but I thought He was going to take Samuel [their eldest boy]."

She exhorted my father to give his heart to God, saying, "I am going to heaven—meet me there."

He had great faith in her prayers and begged her to pray that God would spare her life. "I cannot live without you and raise the children alone!" he cried.

With a heavenly smile upon her face, and with faith unwavering, she said, "God will take care of you and the children. Weep not for me; I am going to glory!" Then she added, "Never touch liquor anymore!" He promised her he would not. Then she exhorted us all to meet her in heaven.

Suddenly, she shouted aloud and praised God, saying, "Oh, I can see the angels all in the room. Can't you see them?"

At her request, we sang "I Saw a Wayworn Traveler" and "Oh, Come Angel Band." She joined with us, and, while singing the last song, her spirit went home to God.

From the time of Mother's death, our father kept his vow. He erected a family altar and taught us six children, both by example and precept, to trust in our mother's God and to meet her in heaven. Each morning and evening, he would take us to God in prayer around the family altar, and, five years after mother's death, he, too, died in the triumphs of faith and went to heaven.

—Shaw, *Dying Testimonies of Saved and Unsaved*

# "The Angels Say There Is Plenty of Room Up There"

*An account of her sister's death, as told by Kate H. Booth of Buffalo, New York*

My sister was a devoted Christian, and to show the depth of her piety, I shall first quote from her diary:

> Friday, August 22—I consecrated myself anew to follow God. The fire came down and consumed the sacrifice. All was put on the altar and remains there.
>
> Tuesday, August 26—I received such a baptism as I never received before, and, today, I say, "Anyway, Jesus, only glorify Thyself."
>
> Give joy or grief, give ease or pain,
> Take life or friends away,
> But let me find them all again,
> In that eternal day.[19]

"Sudden death would be sudden glory," she proclaimed.

She was constantly praising the Lord for His mercy and grace and was thankful for every kindness shown. Some of her expressions were, "It's all right; it is all clear. Death has lost its sting. I am almost there."

19. Charles Wesley, "And Let This Feeble Body Fail," 1759.

One evening, while the sun was setting and the autumn leaves were tinged with a golden hue, she quoted Psalm 23:4: "'*Yea, though I walk through the valley of the shadow of death, I will fear no evil: for thou art with me; thy rod and thy staff they comfort me.*'"

One day, she had a vision of the unseen world. Her face became radiant with a divine glow, and it seemed as though she was about to leave us.

I called, "Oh, Jennie, what are your last words?"

She revived and said, "Be true. But what made you call me back?"

I asked, "What did you see?"

"It's all right there," she replied, then waved her hand in token of victory.

During her illness, she often expressed her desire that she might retain consciousness to the last, and she requested all of us to pray that this wish might be fulfilled. Her desire was granted, and, in full possession of her faculties, she came to the river's brink.

As the end neared, she would repeat the lines:

> Labor is rest, and pain is sweet,
> If Thou, my God, art here.[20]

On one occasion, she asked me to read the hymn "How Blest the Righteous When He Dies." She thought it so beautiful that she requested it be sung at her funeral.

On Tuesday night, she said, "It is a hard struggle tonight, but a glorious victory tomorrow."

Wednesday was her last day on earth—a bright and glorious one, too, for she felt she was soon to enter the presence of her Lord. It was the first of October and her father's birthday.

In the evening, just an hour or two before the end, the doctor came in. She looked up at him with a smile and said, "Doctor, how am I?" The tears were coursing down his cheeks when she added, "The angels say there is plenty of room up there!"

—Shaw, *Dying Testimonies of Saved and Unsaved*

---

20. Charles Wesley, "Talk with Us, Lord," 1740.

# "Till Morning"

*Through the kindness of Dr. L. B. Balliett of Allentown, Pennsylvania, comes the following incident:*

The last words of noted actor Edward Adams were, "Good-bye, Mary; good-bye forever!"

What a contrast to one of the martyrs, who, while going to the stake, said to his wife, "Good-bye, Mary, till morning!"

The next morning, this Mary—the martyr's wife—while being put into a sack to be thrown into a pond, handed her babe to a kind neighbor and said, "Good-bye, children! Good-bye, friends! I go to my husband. We will soon meet again. Christ lights the way!"

—Shaw, *Dying Testimonies of Saved and Unsaved*

# "I Am Damned to All Eternity"

*Adapted from an article by Rev. Thomas Graham*

When I was holding a meeting in Middlesex, Pennsylvania, in 1843, a man named Edwards died. He had killed a hog, and, while preparing the sausages, he took some of the ground pepper and, in fun, attempted to make some friends sneeze. One of the company succeeded in doing the same to him, causing him to sneeze twice, breaking a blood vessel.

The doctor was sent for, but to no avail. The rupture was so far into his head, nothing could be done for him. When he was told that he must die, he shrieked so that he could be heard almost a mile away. He cried, "Then I am damned for all eternity!" and continued this fearful exclamation until he died.

—Shaw, *Dying Testimonies of Saved and Unsaved*

# "Tell Alan I Still Have Faith in Him"

*Submitted by Alan Williams of Benton Harbor, Michigan*

My mother professed Christianity, but she was, all her lifetime, in bondage to the fear of death. Although a denominational church member, I was an alcoholic for many years, even estranged from all family contact for seven years. It was during this period that Mother died.

Before she died, she had become justified by faith in our Lord Jesus Christ and had found peace with God, leaving this message for me, "Tell Alan I still have faith in him."

Three years later, Jesus Christ, God's dear Son, set me free from alcohol, and I am "*free indeed*" (John 8:36). As a child of God for seven years now, I have been led by the Holy Spirit to be a witness to Jesus my Lord. Once, God led me to send a postcard message to a seventy-year-old man who had been a lifetime church member and was now on his deathbed.

In the postcard, I wrote, "Our weaknesses and inabilities are inconsequential, since Jesus Christ is our strength and peace. However, the joy of the Holy Ghost comes when we decide to dedicate our all to God's service."

The Spirit Himself then bore witness with this dying man's spirit that he was a child of God and was saved. Before he died, he made this statement: "Tell Alan it's all right now. I believe and understand it all." Then, he gave his first smile of true joy, and he was gone shortly thereafter.

# Mother Cobb (1853)

The beloved Eunice Cobb, better known as "Mother Cobb," was born February 13, 1793, at Litchfield, Connecticut. Mother Cobb was converted when twenty-four, and, after she had walked with God on earth for sixty years, He took her to Himself to reign with Him forever in the courts above.

We select the following from an account of her life and death, published in the *Marengo Republican*:

> During a pilgrimage of forty years with this people, she ever exhibited an earnest zeal in the service of her Lord and Master. To her, religion was more than a name—a profession. It was a reality, a power, revealed in the heart that led, controlled, and adorned her whole life and being. She stopped at the fountain, not only to drink but also to wash and be made whiter than snow.
>
> Filled with holy enthusiasm for the salvation of souls, she devoted a large portion of her time to this work, visiting from house to house and talking and praying with all with whom she came in contact. No work was so pressing as to take away time for prayer; no public worship so imposing as to dissuade her from giving the most tender and thrilling appeals to the unconverted to accept Christ and exhorting the believers to a higher, holier life. She was truly a godly woman, abundant in labors and in fruits.
>
> Mother Cobb loved everybody, regardless of name or sect. Though fallen asleep, she yet lives in the hearts of those who have been saved by her instrumentality or blessed by her counsel. We have no words that can do full justice to the eminently devoted Christian life and character of this mother in Israel. It has been fittingly said that her life is a grand commentary on the thirteenth chapter of 1 Corinthians, and this, to those who knew her, will be the most appropriate testimony for her Christian worth—the best epitaph that can be inscribed to her memory.

Many friends called to see her, and to all, she testified to her perfect faith in Christ and of His grace, not only to sustain but also to cheer in a dying hour. Heaven itself seemed open to her, and a holy ecstasy filled her soul. Her last words were, "Victory! Victory! Eternal victory!"

—Shaw, *Dying Testimonies of Saved and Unsaved*

# Sylvia Marie Torres (1966)

*Submitted by Mrs. Ralph F. Becker of Holland, New York*

Our precious, talented, and lovely granddaughter fell asleep in Jesus just before Christmas at the age of nine. It was so hard to put that little body of clay into the ground. But it will come forth in the morning, when the day breaks and the shadows flee away.

She spent many weeks in such intense suffering that an adult dose of morphine was not able to help. She said she knew how the Lord Jesus suffered for her.

"Only He suffered more," she said.

When her knees and wrists were dreadfully swollen and painful, she said she knew how the Lord felt when they put nails through His hands and feet. On her final trip to the hospital, she said, "If the Lord wants me to go back, I am not going to make a fuss anymore but just ask Him for grace to bear the pain."

One day, she was so miserable, and her father was leaning over her, trying to stop her nose from bleeding, as he softly sang to her. She said, "Daddy, don't sing, because you get my song all mixed up." When he said that he didn't know she was singing, she replied that she wasn't singing out loud. Earlier, she had asked him for help with the words to "Blessed Assurance." No doubt, she was singing that song.

Another time, she asked her father if the pain would stop as soon as she got to heaven.

Just a few hours before she died, she murmured, "Yes, Lord Jesus." Then, a little later, she spoke the same words: "Yes, Lord Jesus." We were praying that the Lord would be near and precious to her, and we know He was.

After she was gone, her mother found a little paper pinned to the wall behind a curtain in her room. On it, she had printed these words: "Have Thine own way, Lord."

Her doctor said she was truly a saint. Another said, "I have heard about the Lord, but now I have seen Him in a little girl." Someone else declared, "She has taught me more in a few short years than I have learned in the past forty."

# Joan of Arc (1431)

This French heroine, "The Maid of Orleans," is described as having been of a sweet, sympathetic nature yet being endowed with heroic patriotism. She grew up as a peasant girl, strong and beautiful and imbued with the fervor of her faith. She claimed to have had heavenly visions and revelations from angels, who pointed out her mission to rescue her people from English domination. In this undertaking, she successfully became a renowned military leader who led French forces to many victories in battle during the Hundred Years' War.

Finally, at the tender age of nineteen, she was captured by the Burgundians and sold to the English, who condemned her to be burned to death for heresy. All the tortures that the age knew, all the cruel thrusts at the sensitive flesh, were tried on her!

Her inquisitors hurled their demands: "Say but that thy voices were false, fair maid. Pronounce thy spirit guides to have been delusions, and thou shalt escape the coming doom."

All persuasion was in vain, however, and her voice rang out amid the flames: "Yes, my voices were from God! They have never deceived me! Jesus!"

—Shaw, *Dying Testimonies of Saved and Unsaved*

# Ann Audebert
## (1549)

Ann Audebert was the widow of a French apothecary. She was martyred by burning in 1549.

When the rope was put about her waist, she called it her "wedding girdle" wherewith she would be married to Christ. As the fires were lit, she said, "Upon a Saturday I was first married, and upon a Saturday I shall be married again!"

—Gottschall, *Selections from Testimonies and Dying Words*

# Maria Jane Taylor
## (1870)

*Wife of J. Hudson Taylor*

The birth of their last child, Noel, was the occasion of the home-going of this precious saint of God—wife and fellow laborer of that prince of missionary heroes, J. Hudson Taylor. We quote from the well-known biography of Mr. Hudson Taylor, written by his son and daughter-in-law, who were also devoted missionaries to China:

> Born on the 7th of July, this little one was their fifth son and called forth all the pent-up love of his parents' hearts.
>
> "How graciously the Lord has dealt with me and mine," Mr. Taylor wrote home afterwards. "How tenderly did He bring my loved one through the hour of trial and gave us our last-born, our Noel. How I thanked Him as I stroked the soft, silky hair and nestled the little one in my bosom! And how she loved him when, with a father's joy and pride,

I brought him to her for her first kiss, and together we gave him to the Lord."

But an attack of cholera had greatly prostrated the mother, and lack of natural nourishment told upon the child. When a Chinese nurse could be found, it was too late to save the little life. After one brief week on earth, he went back to the home above, in which his mother was so soon to join him.

"Though excessively prostrate in body," Mr. Taylor wrote in the same letter, "the deep peace of soul, the realization of the Lord's own presence, and the joy in His holy will with which she was filled, and in which I was permitted to share, I can find no words to describe."

She herself chose the hymns to be sung at the little grave, one of which, "O Holy Savior, Friend Unseen," seemed especially to dwell in her mind.

Weak as she was, it had not yet occurred to them that for her, too, the end was near. The deep mutual love that bound their hearts in one seemed to preclude the thought of separation. And she was only thirty-three. There was no pain up to the very last, though she was weary, very weary.

A letter from Mrs. Berger in England had been received two days previously, telling of the safe arrival at Saint Hill of Miss Blatchley and the Taylors' children. Every detail of the welcome and arrangements for their well-being filled her heart with joy. She knew not how to be thankful enough and seemed to have no desire or heart but just to praise the Lord for His goodness.

Many and many a time had Mrs. Berger's letters reached their destination at the needed moment; many and many a time had her loving heart anticipated the circumstances in which they would be received—but never more so than with this letter.

"And now farewell, precious friend," she wrote. "The Lord throw around you His everlasting arms!"

It was in those arms she was resting.

At daybreak on Saturday, the 23rd of July, she was sleeping quietly, and Mr. Taylor left her a few moments to prepare some food. While he was doing so, she awoke, and serious symptoms called him to her side.

"By this time, it was dawn," he wrote, "and the sunlight revealed what the candle had hidden—the deathlike hue of her countenance. Even my love could no longer deny, not her danger, but that she was actually dying. As soon as I was sufficiently composed, I said, 'My darling, do you know that you are dying?'

"'Dying!' she replied. 'Do you think so? What makes you think so?'

"I said, 'I can see it, darling. Your strength is giving way.'

"'Can it be so? I feel no pain, only weariness.'

"'Yes, you are going home. You will soon be with Jesus.'

"My precious wife thought of my being left alone at a time of so much trial, with no companion like herself, with whom I had been wont to bring every difficulty to the throne of grace.

"'I am so sorry,' she said, then paused, as if half correcting herself for the feeling.

"'You are sorry to go to be with Jesus?'

"Never shall I forget the look with which she answered.

"'Oh, no! It is not that. You know, darling, that for ten years past, there has not been a cloud between me and my Savior. I cannot be sorry to go to Him, but it does grieve me to leave you alone at such a time. Yet, He will be with you and meet all your need.'"

But little was said after that. A few loving messages to those at home, a few last words about the children, and she seemed to fall asleep or drift into unconsciousness of earthly things. The summer sun rose higher and higher over the city, the hills, and the river. The busy hum of life came up around them from many a court and street. But, within one Chinese dwelling, in an upper room from which the blue of God's own heaven could be seen, there was the hush of a wonderful peace.

"I never witnessed such a scene," wrote Mrs. Duncan a few days later. "As dear Mrs. Taylor was breathing her last, Mr. Taylor knelt down—his heart so full—and committed her to the Lord, thanking Him for having given her and for the twelve-and-a-half years of happiness they had had together; thanking Him, too, for taking her to His own blessed presence, and solemnly dedicating himself anew to His service."

It was just after 9 a.m. when the quiet breathing ceased, and they knew she was *"with Christ, which is far better"* (Philippians 1:23).

—Dr. and Mrs. Howard Taylor, *Hudson Taylor and the China Inland Mission* (1927)

# Samuel Rutherford (1661)

This eminent Scotch Presbyterian was born in 1600 and died in 1661. He was commissioner to the Westminster General Assembly in 1643 and was, for some time, principal of St. Andrews College.

When on his deathbed, he was summoned to appear before Parliament to stand trial for having preached "Liberty and Religion." He sent word with the messenger: "Tell the Parliament that I have received a summons to a higher bar—I must needs answer that, first. When the day you name comes, I shall be where few of you shall enter."

—Shaw, *Dying Testimonies of Saved and Unsaved*

# Peter of Lampsacus (c. 251)

Accused before the proconsul Optimus of Christian faith, Peter of Lampsacus was ordered to sacrifice to the goddess Venus. To this, he replied, "I am astonished that you should command me to worship a woman who, according to your own history, was a vile and licentious character, and guilty of such crimes as your own laws now punish with death. No, instead I shall offer to the one living and true God the sacrifice of prayer and praise!"

For this statement, his bones were torn apart on a rack, his head cut off, and his body given to the dogs.

—Gottschall, *Selections from Testimonies and Dying Words*

# David Brainerd
# (1747)

This celebrated missionary to the Native Americans was born April 20, 1718, at Haddam, Connecticut. His parents were noted for their piety and were closely related to high officials of the church and state.

In 1739, he entered Yale College, where he stood first in his class. He was greatly favored of God in being privileged to attend the great revival conducted by George Whitefield, Jonathan Edwards, and Gilbert Tennent.

Edwards says in his memoir of Brainerd,

> His great work was the priceless example of his piety, zeal, and self devotion. Why, since the days of the apostles, none has surpassed him. His uncommon intellectual gifts, his fine personal qualities, his melancholy, and his early death, as well as his remarkable holiness and evangelistic labors, have conspired to invest his memory with a book halo.
>
> The story of his life has been a potent force in the modern missionary era. It is even related that Henry Martyn, while perusing the life of David Brainerd, found his soul filled with a holy emulation of that extraordinary man, and, after deep consideration and fervent prayer, he was, at length, fixed in a resolution to imitate his example.

Brainerd was a representative man, formed both by nature and grace to leave a lasting impression upon the piety of the church. He died October 9, 1747, at

Northampton. The last words of this eminent apostle were these: "I am almost in eternity; I long to be there. My work is done. I have done with my friends—all the world is nothing to me. Oh, to be in heaven to praise and glorify God with His holy angels!"

—Shaw, *Dying Testimonies of Saved and Unsaved*

# Hattie Buford (1865)

This little girl, the daughter of Major General John Buford, died in 1865 at the age of six. She had been taught to repeat the Lord's Prayer, and, as she lay dying, all of a sudden, she opened her soft blue eyes and, looking confidently into her mother's face, said, "Mama, I forgot to say my prayers!"

Summoning what strength she had left, she clasped her little hands together and, like a little angel, prayed thus:

Now I lay me down to sleep,
I pray Thee, Lord, my soul to keep;
If I should die before I wake,
I pray Thee, Lord, my soul to take.

The prayer finished, she never spoke again.

—Shaw, *Dying Testimonies of Saved and Unsaved*

# Margareta Klopstock (1758)

Friedrich Klopstock was a German poet, author of the well-known epic poem *Der Messias* [The Messiah]. His wife, Margareta, was a devoted Christian.

In her last moments, Margareta, being told that God would help her, replied, "Yes—into heaven!"

The last words she whispered included a quote from 1 John 1:7: "'*The blood of Jesus Christ...cleanseth from all sin!*' Oh, sweet words of eternal life!"

—Shaw, *Dying Testimonies of Saved and Unsaved*

# Dr. A. J. Gordon (1895)

For many years, Rev. Adoniram Judson Gordon served as pastor of Clarendon Street Baptist Church in Boston, Massachusetts. He was a noted author, as well as publisher of a monthly periodical, *The Watchword*.

According to the memorial notice in *The Watchword*:

> A short time before his death, he called his wife to his side and said, "If anything should happen, I have selected four hymns I want to have sung. Write them down: 'Abide with Me,' 'The Sands of Time Are Sinking,' 'Lord, If He Sleep, He Shall Do Well,' and 'My Jesus, I Love Thee.'"
>
> He was assured that his wishes would be regarded, and the subject was dropped.

At 5:00 p.m., the doctor sat by him and, speaking with a cheery voice to rouse him, said, "Have you a good word for us tonight?" With a clear, full voice, Dr. Gordon answered, "Victory!"

This was his last audible utterance.

Between nine and ten in the evening, the nurse motioned to his wife that she was wanted. She bent to listen as he whispered, "Maria, pray!" As she led in prayer, he followed in a whisper, sentence by sentence, and, at the close, tried to utter petitions himself. However, his strength was not sufficient to articulate.

Five minutes after midnight on the morning of February 2, he fell asleep in Jesus.

—Shaw, *Dying Testimonies of Saved and Unsaved*

# A Dying Welsh Soldier's Despair

*From* Crown of Glory, *author unknown*

I once went to visit a soldier who had brought himself from the army. He was dying but did not know it. I sat down by his side and said, "I will read a bit of the Bible for you."

"Oh, you need not trouble; I am not so ill as all that," he replied.

Poor fellow. He thought that he must be very ill before anyone need offer to read a part of the Bible for him.

Next morning, when I called, I found him in much worse shape. I learned that he was a Welshman and his mother was a Christian. Suddenly, he threw himself back in bed. Wringing his hands, he cried, "Oh, what shall I do, what shall I do? I am as a dead man. The mark of death is upon me, and I am not saved!"

There is a time when God speaks and Christ may be found, but there is also a time when He may not be found. This young dying soldier sought and sought for Christ, but it was all in vain—Jesus had passed by. He finally became delirious and died in agony.

> *Seek ye the* Lord *while he may be found, call ye upon him while he is near.*
> (Isaiah 55:6)

—Shaw, *Dying Testimonies of Saved and Unsaved*

# A Little Girl's Glimpse into Eternity

Mrs. William Barnes's wonderful conversion was brought about by the death of her little girl. The following is her own story of the child's passing:

> My little daughter, May, when but eight years old, was taken ill with scarlet fever and died four days later. During her short sickness, when asked if she was suffering, she would say that nothing hurt her, but that she did not want to stay with us any longer—she wanted to go to heaven. She kept repeating this all through the long night.
>
> Toward the end, she repeated the Lord's Prayer and then sweetly thanked us for all that we had done for her, insisting that we should not worry about her. Suddenly, she looked up and said, "I thank Thee, dear Jesus. Dear Jesus, I thank Thee!"
>
> After that, she sang some beautiful songs.
>
> Just before she died, she raised her eyes toward heaven and said, "O Lord, my strength and my Redeemer." Then, with a peaceful look on her face, she raised herself and, with a glad expression, said, "Oh!" and was gone. It was evident that she saw something that our eyes could not see.

I think this message, dear reader, is for you, just as much as it is for me. The Bible says, *"A little child shall lead them"* (Isaiah 11:6).

—Shaw, *Dying Testimonies of Saved and Unsaved*

# "Oh, the Devil Is Coming to Drag My Soul Down to Hell!"

*As told by N. M. Nelms of Kopperl, Texas*

Miss A— was taken very sick and was informed that she could not live. Her parents had educated her to follow the ways and fashions of the world and had turned her away from the truth of God. Now, she lay dying, surrounded by her young friends, with whom she had indulged in the pleasures of sin.

The wretched girl called her father to the bedside and, in front of everybody, said, "Your heart is as black as hell. If you had taught me to live for God, rather than spending your time quarreling with Mother, I might have been saved."

Turning to others, she pled with them, saying, "Do not follow my ungodly example. Do not do as I have done. Do not indulge in the hellish pleasures of the world! Oh, if I had only heeded the warnings...."

Then, she suddenly cried, "Oh, the devil is coming to drag my soul down to hell! I am lost, lost forever!"

Then she died.

—Shaw, *Dying Testimonies of Saved and Unsaved*

# Merritt Caldwell (1848)

This great and good man, principal of Wesleyan Academy in Maine and vice president of Dickinson College in Pennsylvania, was a gifted writer. He was born in 1806 and died in 1848.

Shortly before his death, he said to his wife, "You will not, I am sure, lie down upon your bed and weep when I am gone. You will not mourn for me when God has been so good to me. When you visit my grave, do not come in the shade of the evening, nor in the dark of night—these are no times to visit the grave of a Christian—but come in the morning, in the bright sunshine, when the birds are singing."

His last expression was, "Glory to Jesus! He is my trust; He is my strength! Jesus lives; I shall live also!"

—Shaw, *Dying Testimonies of Saved and Unsaved*

# Count Zinzendorf of the Moravians (1760)

*German Religious and Social Reformer; Bishop of the Moravian Church*

To his family and friends, the dying saint triumphantly said, "I am going to my Savior. I am ready. There is nothing to hinder me now. I cannot say how much I love you all. Who would have believed that the prayer of Christ *'that they all may be one'* could have been so strikingly fulfilled among us! I only asked for firstfruits among the heathen, and thousands have been given me. Are we not as in heaven! Do we not live together like the angels! The Lord and His servants understand each other. I am ready."

A few hours later, his son-in-law pronounced the Old Testament benediction: "*'The Lord bless thee, and keep thee: the Lord make his face shine upon thee, and be gracious unto thee: the Lord lift up his countenance upon thee, and give thee peace*'" (Numbers 6:24–26). Then, this dear man of God fell asleep in Jesus and was absent from the body and at home with his Lord.

# "I See Two Angels Coming for Me"

*Submitted by Mr. Y. Courvoisier of Switzerland*

In regard to your book *Voices from the Edge of Eternity*, I have in my possession a letter from my grandmother, written in 1873. She writes about the wife of Pastor Bernard, who was the pastor of the French Church in Bern, Switzerland.

This Pastor Bernard was the one who instructed my mother. He was a true believer, and at that time, many were converted to Christianity through him.

I quote from this letter: "Mme. Bernard died after very much suffering from neuralgia-asthma and at last dropsy. What a sad time for the poor girls, to say nothing of the pastor himself. The end was very peaceful, and nearly her last words were, 'I see two angels coming for me.'"

# "I Cannot Be Pardoned; It Is Too Late! Too Late!"

*Submitted by Rev. E. Phelps, D.D.*

> *Because I have called, and ye refused; I have stretched out my hand, and no man regarded…I also will laugh at your calamity; I will mock when your fear cometh….Then shall they call upon me, but I will not answer; they shall seek me early, but they shall not find me: for that they hated knowledge, and did not choose the fear of the* Lord. (Proverbs 1:24, 26, 28–29)

Miss— was an amiable young girl who died at the age of sixteen. She was the daughter of respectable and pious parents in one of the New England states. Considerable attention had been bestowed on the cultivation of her mind, but to what extent she had been imbued with Christian truth in childhood, I have not been able fully to learn. It is certain that from her earliest years she had regarded religion with respect and expected to become a Christian before she died.

One morning in particular, the first impression she had when she awoke was that she must receive Christ then—that her soul was in imminent danger of being lost if she delayed. She deliberated and reasoned. Finally, she prayed and made a deliberate resolution that she would repent and accept God's offer of salvation before the close of that day. However, the day had its cares and pleasures. Activity and company filled its hours, and the night found her almost as thoughtless as she had been for months.

The next morning, this spiritual impression was renewed and deepened. The violated vows of the previous morning gave her some uneasiness, but she now formed her resolution firmly and was so fixed in her purpose that she felt sure everything would be all right. The agony of her soul gave way to the soothing reflection that she should soon be a Christian. She had now taken—as she imagined—"one step." She had formed a solemn purpose and had given a pledge to repent that day. She felt, as she expressed it, "committed," and she hardly had a doubt as to the accomplishment of her purpose.

But this day also passed as before. She did, indeed, several times during the day, think of her resolution, but not with that overwhelming interest she had felt in the morning, and nothing decisive was done.

The next morning, God again spoke to her heart, and she again renewed her resolution, only to have it dissipated as before. Thus, she went on resolving and breaking her resolutions, until, at length, her anxiety entirely subsided, and she lapsed into her former state of unconcern.

It was not that she became completely indifferent. She still expected and resolved to be a Christian; but her resolutions now looked to a more distant period for their accomplishment, and she returned to the cares and pleasures of the world with the same interest as before.

About this time, she went to reside in a neighboring village, and I did not see her for about three months. Suddenly, I was called at an early hour to visit her on the bed of death.

About daybreak, on the morning of the day she died, she was informed that her symptoms had become alarming and that her sickness would probably be fatal. Her intelligence was surprising, and though she sought desperately to "find God," her distress became so intense, and her energies so exhausted, that she finally was forced to conclude that her soul was lost and that nothing could now be done. For a moment, she seemed as if in a horrid struggle to adjust her mind to her anticipated doom. Oh, that word *lost*. Her whole frame shuddered at the thought.

It was nearly noon. Most of the morning had been employed either in prayer at her bedside or in attempting to guide her to the Savior. But all seemed ineffectual. Her strength was now nearly gone. Vital action was no longer perceptible at the extremities, the cold death-sweat was gathering on her brow, and dread despair seemed ready to possess her soul.

She saw, and we all saw, that the fatal moment was at hand, and her future prospect one of unmingled horror. She shrank from it. Turning her eyes to me, she called on all who stood around her to beseech once more the God of mercy in her behalf.

We all knelt again at her bedside, and, having once more commended her to God, I tried again to direct her to the Savior. I was beginning to repeat some promises which I thought appropriate when she interrupted me, saying, with emphasis, "I cannot be pardoned; it is too late! Too late!"

Alluding to her vain and fatal resolutions, she begged me to charge all the youth of my congregation not to neglect salvation as she had done—not to stifle their conviction by a mere resolution to repent.

"Warn them, warn them by my case," she said.

After that, she again attempted to pray but only fainted. She continued thus, alternately to struggle and faint, every succeeding effort becoming feebler, until the last convulsive struggle closed the scene, and her spirit took its everlasting flight.

The Bible says that *"man looketh on the outward appearance, but the* LORD *looketh on the heart"* (1 Samuel 16:7).

> *Keep thy heart with all diligence; for out of it are the issues of life.*
> (Proverbs 4:23)

—Shaw, *Dying Testimonies of Saved and Unsaved*

# The Awful End of a Scoffer

*Submitted by Rev. Fredrick Scott*

In the year 1880, several of us held a little street meeting off Brightside Lane, Sheffield, England, our object being to extend an invitation to passersby to come to the services at the Primitive Methodist Chapel, which was nearby.

We stopped on the street, close to the home of the subject of this sketch (whose name I do not remember), and commenced to sing and talk to the people. Suddenly, this man came out of his house in a great rage, saying that we were disturbing the peace and ought to be prosecuted. He caught the attention of some of the people and told them that the Bible was a humbug, Christianity a fraud, and churches and ministers an imposition on the people. He declared that society should be rid of them all. We endeavored to reason with him, but it was in vain.

The following week, some of the Christians called at his home and offered to pray with him and provide some literature, but he scornfully refused all their offers. Abusing their good intentions, he criticized the narrowness of Christianity and boasted of the great freedom of infidelity.

Several times after that, he made a point of meeting us on the street, endeavoring to confuse the people and break up our meeting. His presence was such an annoyance to us, and so detrimental to the meetings, that we could scarcely hold them.

The last time he tried to interfere was on a Sunday morning. He came walking down the street with a large stick in one hand and an ax in the other. We were singing, and, as soon as he got close, he began to chop the wood. Of course, he wanted to draw the attention of the people away from us. The chips began to fly around, and we thought it best to move on.

From that time, we all began to offer special prayer for his conversion. However, God did not answer our prayers in the way we thought He would. The next Sunday, we went to our street meeting feeling that, in some way, God would give us a victory over the man, but, to our surprise, he did not turn up. I inquired about him and found that he had become very ill.

The following week, I was called to his room and found him in a very dangerous condition. He was much changed in his mind and very mild, tender, and teachable. But he could not repent. Many Christians visited him and tried to lead him to Jesus, but their efforts were all in vain. He said that he knew he was lost and doomed forever.

In a few days, I called again and found him very close to the crossing. I told him of God's boundless mercy and how it had reached even Nebuchadnezzar (see Daniel 4) and Manasseh (see 2 Chronicles 33) and that God had given His Son for him, also. His answer was simply to insist that it was too late, since he had sinned against light and knowledge when he had known better. The fact of having disturbed our meetings weighed on his mind, and he told me to faithfully warn all such scoffers of their danger. He wept bitterly as we talked to him of his lost condition, and he said that if he could only live his life over again, he would live for God. But it was a vain hope. Life was now past and his last chance gone.

The distress of his mind became worse and worse as the end approached, and he finally died in great agony of soul.

To live without Christ is only to exist, missing the whole point of life. To be without Christ on a deathbed is terrible. To go into eternity without Christ is midnight, darkness forever. Oh, the thought of an eternity without Christ!

—Shaw, *Dying Testimonies of Saved and Unsaved*

# Rev. Hiram Case

*Submitted by his wife, Mrs. Gertrude M. Case, of Clyde, New York*

A few weeks before his death, my husband, Rev. Hiram Case, said, "It seemed as if I were stepping into a very cold stream, which sent a shiver through my entire being. In the twinkling of an eye, however, the place was lit up with a glory that far outshone the noonday sun. What I saw and felt was unutterable. Words are too lame to express what I saw and felt of the presence of the Lord with me."

My husband had some relatives who were Adventists. He wished they could know how he felt when he knew he was dying. They would never again think that their spirits sleep in the grave until the resurrection but would know beyond a doubt that, immediately after the spirit leaves the body, it is with the redeemed host in a conscious existence in the presence of the great Redeemer of men.

He talked freely about dying, saying that, while it was hard to part with us—the family—the Lord knew what was best. At another time, he heard the heavenly music. He said, "Hear that music! They don't have such music as that on earth."

The presence of the Lord was with him during all these trying days, and, when the power of speech and sight was gone, by the pressure of the hand and the farewell kiss, he gave us the token that all is well!

—Shaw, *Dying Testimonies of Saved and Unsaved*

# Edward Gibbon (1794)

*Noted English Historian and Parliamentarian; Author of* The History of the Decline and Fall of the Roman Empire

Bishop John Fletcher Hurst, in *History of Rationalism,* wrote of Gibbon,

> By a sudden caprice he became a Roman Catholic, and afterwards as unceremoniously denied his adopted creed....In due time he found himself in Paris publishing a book in the French language. He there fell in with the fashionable infidelity and so yielded to the flattery of Helvetius and all the frequenters of Holbach's house that he jested at Christianity and assailed its divine character.
>
> He has left less on record against Christianity than Hume, but they must be ranked together as the last of the family of English Deists.

Rev. E. P. Goodwin, in *Christianity and Infidelity,* summarized Gibbon's life as one of the fairest, as well as one of the ablest, of infidels. He pointed out that Gibbon has given us an autobiographical account in which, amid all the polish and splendor of the rhetoric of which he is such a master, there is not a line or a word that suggests reverence for God; not a word of regard for the welfare of the human race; nothing but the most sordid selfishness, vainglory, desire for admiration, adulation of the great and wealthy, contempt for the poor, and supreme devotedness to his own gratification.

Gibbon died in 1794 in London. His last words were, "All is now lost—finally, irrecoverably lost. All is dark and doubtful."

—Shaw, *Dying Testimonies of Saved and Unsaved*

# Susan C. Kirtland
# (1864)

*Adapted from an article by Mrs. Etta E. Sadler Shaw*

*Precious in the sight of the Lord is the death of his saints.* (Psalm 116:15)

At a very early age, Mrs. Susan C. Kirtland gave her heart to God. Though her life seemed full of privation and disappointment, she was a cheerful, devoted Christian, well described by the motto she so often expressed in words: "It is better to suffer wrong than to do wrong."

While visiting at our home in Burr Oak, Michigan, she became ill and, after one painful week, went to be with the Lord on April 3, 1864.

At the time, I was less than four years old, but I distinctly remember how, while lying there in great suffering, she taught me the beautiful verse: *"I love them that love me; and those that seek me early shall find me"* (Proverbs 8:17), carefully explaining the meaning of the words and lovingly pressing home the lesson to my heart.

As soon as it was known that she was dangerously ill, her brother, who was an able physician, was summoned. But it was too late.

A few hours before her death, she sensed from Mother's manner that something was wrong and inquired. With much feeling, Mother answered, "Susan, we fear your stay with us is very short."

Calmly, she replied, "Well, if it be so, I don't know when I could have had a better time to leave this stage of action!"

Two of her four children were with her. While they stood weeping by her bedside, she tenderly and earnestly exhorted them to live for God and to meet her in heaven, also sending loving messages to the other two who were absent. Then she bade good-bye to all the friends who were present. No other preparation was needed; she was ready to go.

As the circle of those who loved her so dearly watched around her bed, her face lighted up with indescribable joy as she evidently caught sight of things hidden from others' eyes. Eagerly raising both hands while still looking upward, she exclaimed in a voice of holy triumph, which no words can describe, "O glory! O glory! O glory!"—and was gone.

To her, there was no dark valley, no gloom. Christ was sufficient as she entered into that *"inheritance incorruptible, and undefiled, and that fadeth not away"* (1 Peter 1:4).

—Shaw, *Dying Testimonies of Saved and Unsaved*

# "Come On, I Am Ready to Go!"

*Submitted by Mrs. Wealthy L. Harter of Fort Wayne, Indiana*

During a wonderful revival meeting, my sister, Filura Clark, nineteen years of age, and myself, two years younger, were saved and found great peace with God. Oh, what happy times we had together after that, living for the Lord while other young people went after the things of the world!

But then my dear sister was taken ill and only lived a few days. How very hard it was to part with her! It seemed as if my heart would break, the blow was so great. Yet what a blessed, happy death. Actually, it was not death to her. She did not think of death, for heaven and eternal life with Jesus completely filled her thoughts as the moments sped along.

She called us, one by one, to her bedside, took our hands, bade us good-bye, and begged us to meet her in heaven. After she had bidden the family farewell, she said to her physician, "Now, Doctor, you come." She bade him good-bye, requesting that he, too, meet her in heaven. He was overcome by the affecting scene.

As we stood there weeping, she said to us, "Don't weep for me. Jesus is with me; I will not have to go alone!" As soon as she said that, she looked up, as though she saw someone waiting for her, and said, "Come on, I am ready to go!"

She actually *wanted* to go; her work on earth was done. Her death had a wonderful influence in the community, especially on the young people. Many turned to the Lord, saying, "Let me die such a death as hers."

Nor can I describe the blessing this experience has meant to me personally over the years. It has strengthened me and helped me to live according to the blessed truths of the Bible! When trials and temptations have arisen, her dying testimony has been the means of bringing my soul nearer to the Lord than it ever had been before. Praise the Lord!

—Shaw, *Dying Testimonies of Saved and Unsaved*

# "There Is No Help for Me!"

*Submitted by Julia E. Strail of Portlandville, New York*

During some meetings several years ago, we experienced a blessed visitation of the Holy Spirit. Among many who were touched by God was a young girl of about seventeen years. All through the meetings, the Holy Spirit strove with her, and I talked with her at different times—but she always resisted.

The last evening of the services, I went to her side. Again she stood, weeping and trembling. I urged her to seek God. She said, "Oh, I cannot, I cannot!"

I replied, "Yes, leave your young friends and come."

But she still said, "Oh, I cannot, I cannot!"

Afterward, she said that the young people would have laughed at her had she gone.

She left the church and went to her boarding place (she was boarding and attending school). Upon entering, she made the remark that she did not go there to get religion but rather to get an education, adding that she could attend to religion afterward, at any time.

That very night, she was taken violently ill and continued to grow worse for one week before passing into eternity.

To the young associates who came to see her, she said, "Oh! I ought to have sought the Lord in that meeting!"

I was with her the last day, and before she died, I tried to point her to the Lamb of God. But her agonizing reply again and again was, "It is too late now. Oh, it is too late now! There is no help for me!"

In this deplorable condition, she passed into eternity.

—Shaw, *Dying Testimonies of Saved and Unsaved*

# Cardinal Jules Mazarin (1661)

*Italian-French Cardinal and Statesman*

Jules Mazarin was born in 1602 in the kingdom of Naples. The greatness of his abilities was conspicuous even in his early years, as he studied the interests of the various states in Italy and the kingdoms of France and Spain. Becoming profoundly skilled in politics, he was introduced to the French cabinet through the influence of Cardinal Richelieu, who made him one of the executors of his will. During the minority of Louis XIV, Mazarin had the charge of public affairs. His station and great abilities, however, excited the envy of the nobility of France, which occasioned a civil war that continued for several years. Mazarin was, at last, forced to flee. A price was set on his head, and his fine library was sold.

However, this disgrace did not long continue, and he returned to the court with even more honor than he had previously enjoyed. His conduct of the affairs of the kingdom was executed with so much ability and success that he obtained the French king's most unreserved confidence.

Although Mazarin was a man of great ambition who pursued with ardor the chase of worldly honors, a short time before his death, he perceived the vanity of this pursuit and lamented the misapplication of his time and talents. He became greatly affected at the prospect of death and the uncertainty of his future condition. Upon one occasion, he cried out, "Oh, my poor soul! What will become of thee? Whither wilt thou go?"

To the queen dowager of France, who came to visit him in his illness, and who had been his friend at court, he said, "Madame, your favors have undone me. Were I to live again I would be a humble monk rather than a courtier."

—Murray, *Power of Religion on the Mind*

# The Death Angel Stood Before Her

*A testimony from Bob Bucher, personal friend of the editor*

When I was only a few months old, my mother, who was a very godly woman, was awakened one night to see an angel standing at the foot of her bed. The angel said he was going to take me, but my mother said, "No, you are not!"

The next morning, she went to my crib and found me very weak and frail. When she lifted my little hand, it just fell back to the bed. She was frightened.

At that time, my father was working for American Express in the little town of Bucyrus, Ohio. He had been called to the ministry but had held back. When he came home for lunch that noon, Mom told him what had happened and said that she thought I was dying.

At once, Dad got on his knees beside the crib and asked God to forgive him, promising that he would obey the call to serve Christ. As soon as he finished the prayer, Mom actually felt the death angel leave the house. She went to see if any change had come over her baby boy. Imagine her joy when she saw that life had already returned and my face was flushed with living blood. I began to cry for food.

From that day, my father preached the gospel and served the Lord with a glad heart until the day of his death. As a layman, I also am serving Christ.

I am thankful that my father said yes. Not only did that "yes" mean a life of ministry on his part, but it also brought him a mantle that fell on me and, later, upon my sons. They, too, know Christ, and one is now serving Him in the U.S. Army.

Yes, I know that Christ has the keys of life and death!

# Helen A. Carpenter

*As told by L. M. F. Baird of Alabama, New York*

Helen A. Carpenter was born in Hamlin, New York. Although sensible to God and deeply conscientious, even as a child, she didn't completely give her heart to God until she was seventeen. Her entire life after that, however, was characterized by unswerving devotion to His cause.

At nineteen, while in teaching school, she caught a severe cold that developed into tuberculosis, which terminated her earthly life at the age of twenty.

During Helen's illness, she rapidly ripened for heaven. The young friends who called on her would say, "One would not think Helen was going to die. She speaks as if she were going on a most delightful journey!"

About a week before the end, her mother, sitting by Helen's couch, became conscious of a most heavenly influence pervading the entire room. It was so powerful that she could scarcely refrain from shouting aloud. She wondered if Helen, on whose countenance rested a pleased expression, felt it, too.

The next day, Helen said, "Ma, you thought I was asleep yesterday while you were sitting by me. I wasn't, and two angels came into the room. The walls did not hinder their coming. It was just like the words to that hymn:

> My spirit loudly sings;
> The holy ones, behold, they come!
> I hear the noise of wings.[21]

21. Jefferson Hascall, "My Latest Sun Is Sinking Fast," 1860.

"It was all true, only I did not hear any noise."

A few evenings later, her mother, observing her to be unusually restless, placed her hand upon Helen's brow and found it damp with the dew of death. She said to her daughter, "Helen, I think you are very near home. Have you any fear?"

"Not a bit," Helen replied. "Call the family so that I may say good-bye to them."

As they gathered around her, Helen bade each one a loving farewell, telling them all she was going to heaven because of the blood of the Lamb and enjoining them to meet her there.

She then said, "I have been thinking of the verse, '*He that spared not his own Son…*'" (Romans 8:32). Her voice began to falter when she got this far, so her mother repeated the rest of it for her. They asked if she would like to have them sing, and she replied, "Sing until I die; sing my soul away!"

For some time, one of her sisters sang the sweet songs of Zion. Then, as the dying girl's eyes closed in death, her sister Mary bent over to catch the last expression. Helen gave a start of delightful surprise, as though she saw something glorious beyond conception, and her happy spirit went to be forever with the Lord. But a look of inexpressible delight remained on her lovely countenance.

She was, by nature, so gentle and retiring that her friends feared she might have some fear when she came to the "*swelling of Jordan*" (Jeremiah 12:5), but the grace of her heavenly Father enabled her to pass joyously in holy triumph to the skies.

Afterward, her sister Mary Carpenter went to the African country of Monrovia as a missionary and died there. While dying, she said, "Living or dying, it's all right."

Thus, she too submitted her will to that of her heavenly Father, whose wisdom saw it better for her to come to heaven than to labor in Africa.

—Shaw, *Dying Testimonies of Saved and Unsaved*

# God Is Mightier than Man

*Submitted by Vera L. Staley of North Bristol, England*

When I was a child, I remember my father taking me to a church in Herfordshire where an infidel was buried. This man had ordered that his tomb be sealed with large stone slabs and high railings put around it. All this was to make it impregnable.

However, as time passed, a tiny bird dropped a seed into a crevice of the stones. That little seed had taken root, and, eventually, the big stone slabs were rent asunder by the tree that had grown there. God is mightier than man!

How it deepened my faith as I stood there and contemplated that sight.

# He Beheld Heaven

*Submitted by Rosalee Mills Appleby,*
*retired Southern Baptist missionary of Canton, Mississippi*

I went to Brazil as a missionary in 1924. During my first nine months in that land, I studied the Portuguese language in Rio de Janeiro, my teacher being a Presbyterian minister named Señor Menezes, who died during those first months of study.

His wife told me that at the hour of death, he called her to him and said, "My dear, I have preached many times on heaven, but I never dreamed of a heaven as beautiful as the one I now behold!"

# Sophia Rubeti
# (1861)

Sophia was a young lady who lived in Highland, Kansas. She was the daughter of a Sac Indian woman and a French-Canadian employee of the American Fur Company who had sought a home among the western Indians. When her parents died in 1851, she was taken, along with her two sisters, to the Iowa Sac & Fox Mission, where she was raised. She became a Presbyterian and died in Highland at the age of eighteen.

After her death, the following verses were found written in her own hand on the inner lid of her Bible:

> Worlds could not bribe me back to tread
> Again life's weary waste;
> To see again my days o'er spread
> With all the gloomy past.
> My home from henceforth is in heaven;
> Earth, sea, and sun adieu!
> All heaven is unfolded to my eyes,
> I have no sight for you.

Just before passing away, she exclaimed, "I hear delightful music. Oh, it is delightful! Listen and I think you can hear it. Jesus is coming! They are coming; raise me up!"

—Gottschall, *Selections from Testimonies and Dying Words*

# "Jesus, Have Mercy on Father"

*Submitted by Dr. L. B. Balliett of Allentown, Pennsylvania*

In a shanty on First Avenue in New York City, little Mary lay dying. She turned toward her mother and said, "Mother, I am dying, but I am not afraid."

"Not afraid to die?" asked her non-Christian mother.

Little Mary replied, "Not when you have Jesus with you, Mother. Oh, Mother, you must love my Savior!"

Soon at the bedside, on bended knees, was her drunken father. The little daughter rested her hand on his head as she repeated three times, at intervals, "Jesus, have mercy on Father!"

Shortly afterward, she was numbered with the angel choir in heaven, and, three months after her death, both of her parents were converted and, from that time, led Christian lives.

—Shaw, *Dying Testimonies of Saved and Unsaved*

# Cardinal Borgia (1507)

Cesare Borgia, a natural son of Pope Alexander VI, was a man of such conduct and character that Machiavelli, in his famous book *The Prince*, referred to him as a pattern to all princes who would act the part of wise and political tyrants. He was made a cardinal, but since this office imposed some restraints upon him, he soon determined to resign in order to have greater scope for practicing the excesses to which his natural ambition and cruelty prompted him.

After this, he was made Duke of Valentinois by Louis XII of France. He was a man of consummate dexterity and finesse and always seemed prepared for every event. However, the reflections he made a short time before his death in 1507 reveal that his wit was confined to the concerns of earth. He obviously had not acted upon that wise and enlarged view of things which becomes a being destined for immortality.

"I have provided," said he, "in the course of my life, for everything except death. Now, alas! I am to die, although entirely unprepared!"

—Murray, *Power of Religion on the Mind*

# Nannie Belle Gilkey (1896)

*Submitted by Sadie A. Cryer of Rockford, Illinois*

Nannie Belle Gilkey died of tuberculosis at the age of twenty. During the intense suffering that came at the close of her illness, she manifested a sweet spirit of patience and proved the truthfulness of God's promise: "*As thy days, so shall thy strength be*" (Deuteronomy 33:25).

When Jesus came for Nannie, He found her waiting and willing to go with Him. For three days before her death, she knew that her time was short, and on the day that she died, she was very happy, singing hymns, such as "Anywhere with Jesus I Can Safely Go" and "I Am So Happy in Jesus."

Once, she said, "Jesus is so near. Do you not feel that He is near, Mama?"

At times, her suffering was intense. Once, she cried, "Oh, what shall I do?"

When told to look to Jesus—that He was the only one who could help her—she looked up, and said, "Yes, Lord!"

Jesus came so near that she exclaimed, "Oh, He is coming, He is coming! Oh, Jesus! Come and take me now—I am ready!"

A few minutes before she left us, Nannie waved her hand and said simply, "Good-bye all." Then, she went to be forever with the Lord.

—Shaw, *Dying Testimonies of Saved and Unsaved*

# Jeanne d'Albret (1572)

*Protestant Queen of Navarre*

This excellent queen was the daughter of Henry II, King of Navarre, and Marguerite de Valois, sister of King François I of France. She was born in the year 1528.

From her childhood, she was carefully educated in the Christian faith, to which she steadfastly adhered all her days. Bishop Burnet said of her "[t]hat she both received the Reformation and brought her subjects to it; that she not only reformed her court, but the whole principality to such a degree that the Golden Age seemed to have returned under her—i.e., Christianity appeared again with its primitive purity and lustre."

Being invited to attend the marriage of her son to the King of France's sister, this illustrious queen fell victim to the cruel plots of the French court against the Protestant religion. Her fortitude and genuine piety did not, however, desert her in this great conflict or at the approach of death.

To some who were about her near the end, she said, "I receive all this as from the hand of God, my most merciful Father—nor have I, during my extremity, feared to die, much less murmured against God for inflicting this chastisement upon me. I knew that whatsoever He does with me, He so orders it that, in the end, it shall turn to my everlasting good."

She expressed some concern for her children, as they would be deprived of her in their tender years, but added, "I doubt not that God Himself will be their Father and Protector, as He has ever been mine in my greatest afflictions. I therefore commit them wholly to His government and fatherly care."

When she saw her ladies and women weeping about her bed, she calmed them, saying, "Weep not for me, I pray you. God, by this sickness, calls me hence to enjoy a better life. I believe that Christ is my only Mediator and Savior, and I look for salvation from no other. I shall now enter into the desired haven, towards which this frail vessel has been a long time steering."

Then, she prayed, "O my God! In Thy good time, deliver me from the troubles of this present life, that I may attain to the felicity which Thou hast promised to bestow upon me."

—Murray, *Power of Religion on the Mind*

**Compiler's Note:** Historians now believe that Jeanne fell ill with a fever before her son's wedding and died within five days. Rumors circulated that she was poisoned by Catherine de Medici because of her Protestant religion, but an autopsy detected no foul play.

# A Young Girl Overcomes Pain and the Fear of Death

*Submitted by T. L. Adams of Magdalena, New Mexico*

In the latter part of the nineteenth century, in Milan, Tennessee, Ella Bledsoe, young daughter of Dr. Bledsoe, lay dying. Being neighbors and fellow Christians, Ella and my sister had been together much of the time and had learned to love each other very tenderly.

Ella had been ill for about nine days. Her Christian father had heretofore kept her under the influence of opiates to ease her pain, but, not willing that she should pass out of this world stupefied by these drugs, he had ceased to administer them.

When my sister, Dorrie, and I heard that Ella was dying, we at once prayed to God that she might not pass away without leaving a dying testimony. We hastened to her bedside and found her tossing from side to side in the painful agonies of the last enemy—death.

My sister approached her and, sitting on the side of the bed, took one of her hands in her own, saying, "Ella, are you afraid to die?"

For a moment, all that life offers to a young girl seemed to rush before her youthful gaze, and she replied, "I hate to die."

Then, turning, like Hezekiah, with her face to the wall for a few moments, doubtless in communion with her heavenly Father, she turned back and said, "Good-bye. I am going to rest." Extending her hand to me, she said, "Good-bye. Meet me at rest."

She then called her family to her bedside, one by one, kissed them, and bade them good-bye, requesting and exhorting them to meet her "where the weary are at rest."

This was an affecting scene which impressed all who were present with the reality of the joy of the Christian experience. When all things around us fade away, Christ enables us to rejoice, even in the face of death. Thank God!

—Shaw, *Dying Testimonies of Saved and Unsaved*

# They Died at Dawn

*Printed in the newsletter* The Pentecostal Evangel *on July 27, 1940*

"One of the strangest experiences in my life is connected with war," said Nordenberg, an eminent engineer in Finland in 1918. "I offered my services to the government and was appointed an officer in General Mannerheim's Army. It was a terrible time. We besieged a town which had been taken by the Red

Army and retook it. A number of Red prisoners were under my guard, and seven of them were to be shot at dawn on Monday. I will never forget the preceding Sunday.

"The seven men were kept in the basement of the Town Hall, and, in the passage, my men stood at attention with their rifles. The atmosphere was filled with hatred. My soldiers were drunk with success and taunted their prisoners. Some of the condemned captives swore and beat on the walls with their bleeding fists; others called for their wives and children who were far away. At dawn, they were all to die.

"We had the victory; that was true enough. But the value of this seemed to diminish as the night advanced. Then, something happened. One of the men doomed to death began to sing.

"*He is mad,* was everybody's first thought. But I had noticed that this man, Koskinen, had not raved and cursed. Quietly, he sat on his bench, a picture of utter despair. Nobody had said anything to him; each was carrying his burden in his own way.

"Koskinen sang rather waveringly at first, then his voice grew stronger and became natural and free. All the prisoners turned and looked at him as he sang:

> Safe in the arms of Jesus,
> Safe on His gentle breast,
> There by His love o'er-shaded,
> Sweetly, my soul shall rest.
> Hark! 'Tis the voice of angels,
> Borne in a song to me,
> Over the fields of jasper,
> Over the jasper sea.[22]

"Over and over again, he sang that verse, and, when he finished, everyone was quiet for a few minutes. Then a wild-looking man broke out with, 'Where did you get that, you fool? Are you trying to make us religious?'

"Koskinen looked at his comrades with tear-filled eyes as he quietly said, 'Comrades, will you listen to me for a minute? You ask me where I got this song. It was from the Salvation Army—I heard it three weeks ago. My mother sang about Jesus and prayed to Him.'

22. Fanny J. Crosby, "Safe in the Arms of Jesus," 1868.

"He stopped a little while, as if to gather strength. Then, he rose to his feet, being the soldier that he was, and looked straight in front of him.

"'It is cowardly to hide your beliefs,' he continued. 'The God my mother believed in is now my God. I cannot tell how it happened, but last night, as I lay awake, I suddenly saw Mother's face before me. It reminded me of the song that I had heard. I felt I had to find the Savior and hide in Him. I prayed that Christ would forgive me, cleanse my sinful soul, and make me ready to stand before Him whom I should meet soon. It was a strange night—there were times when everything seemed to shine around me. Verses from the Bible and the song book came to my mind and brought messages of the crucified Savior and the blood that cleanses from sin—and the home He has prepared for us. I thanked Him, and, since then, this verse has been sounding inside me. It is God's answer to my prayer. I could no longer keep it to myself; within a few hours I shall be with the Lord—saved by grace.'

"Koskinen's face shone as if by an inward light. His comrades sat there quietly. He himself stood there transfixed. My soldiers were also listening to what this Red revolutionary had to say.

"'You are right, Koskinen,' said one of his comrades at last. 'If only I knew there was mercy for me, too, but these hands of mine have shed blood—and I have reviled God and trampled on all that is holy. Now, I realize that there is a hell, and that it is the proper place for me.'

"He sank to the ground with despair on his face.

"'Pray for me, Koskinen,' he groaned. 'Tomorrow, I shall die, and my soul will be in the hands of the devil.'

"These two Red soldiers went down on their knees and prayed for each other. It was no long prayer, but it reached heaven—and we who listened to it forgot our hatred. It melted in the light of heaven, for here were two men who were soon to die seeking reconciliation with their God.

"A door leading into the invisible stood ajar, and we were all entranced by the sight. Let me tell you shortly that by the time it was four o'clock, all Koskinen's comrades had followed his example and begun to pray. The change in the atmosphere was indescribable. Some of them sat on the floor, some on the benches; some wept quietly, and others talked of spiritual things. None of us had a Bible, but the Spirit of God spoke to us all. Then, someone remembered those at home, and there followed an hour of intense letter writing. Confessions and tears were in those letters.

"The night had almost gone and day was dawning, but no one had slept a moment.

"'Sing the song once more for us, Koskinen,' said one of them. And you should have heard them sing—not only that song, but verses and choruses long forgotten. The soldiers on guard united with them, for the power of God had touched all. Everything had changed, and the venerable Town Hall's basement resounded in that early morning hour with the songs of the blood of the Lamb.

"The clock struck six. How I wished I could have begged grace for these men, but I knew that it was impossible. Between two rows of soldiers, they marched out to the place of execution. One of them asked to be allowed to sing Koskinen's song once again, and permission was granted. Then, they asked to be allowed to die with uncovered faces. So, with hands lifted to heaven, they sang with might and main, 'Safe in the Arms of Jesus.'

"When the last line had died out, the lieutenant gave the word: 'Fire!'

"We inclined our heads in silent prayer.

"What happened in the hearts of the others, I do not know, but, as far as I was concerned, I was a new man from that hour. I had met Christ in one of His lowliest and youngest disciples, and I had seen enough to realize that I, too, could be His."

# Legrand d'Alleray
## (1794)

This aged Frenchman and his wife were arraigned before the tribunal during the Reign of Terror, which signified the beginning of the French Revolution. Both were accused of having corresponded with their emigrant son and having assisted him in his exile. The judge hinted at an evasive reply to the charge, which the brave old man declined.

"I thank you for the efforts you make to save me, but it would be necessary to purchase our lives by a lie. My wife and myself prefer rather to die. We have grown old together without ever having lied, and we will not do it now to save a remnant of life."

—Gottschall, *Selections from Testimonies and Dying Words*

# Theodore Parker (1860)

This distinguished American rationalistic lecturer said, "Oh, that I had known the art of life, or found some book or someone had taught me how to live!"

—Gottschall, *Selections from Testimonies and Dying Words*

# "How Beautiful Everything Appears!"

*Submitted by Samuel G. Bingaman of Williams, Oregon*

When I was a soldier in Memphis, Missouri, a comrade once said, "I wish you would go over to that house yonder and stay with them tonight. They are in terrible condition there."

After dark, I went over and did indeed find things in a dreadful state. The house was dilapidated, almost ready to fall down, and the cellar was full of muddy water. I ascended an old pair of stairs on the outside of the house and entered a small room. It contained no furniture, not even chairs or bedsteads, nothing but an old trunk.

On this trunk sat an elderly lady with a little child in her arms. The child was almost dead, and on the floor lay another child that had died only a few minutes before. A third was very low.

The lady pointed to an old pile of dirty bed quilts on the floor in one corner of the room, saying, "There lies the mother, and we don't think she will live until morning. What is worse..."—I thought, *What can be worse?*—"...we are looking for the father to come home tonight drunk."

About midnight, he came; but that awful scene of the dead and dying did not affect the poor drunkard's heart. He drew out his bottle of whiskey and begged me to drink with him!

But there was one of that family who was deeply penitent, earnestly desiring to *"flee from the wrath to come"* (Luke 3:7)—the brokenhearted mother. At her request, I often visited her and would talk to her of the Savior and sing to her of heaven.

One day, while calling to see her, I found her cold and sinking fast. Death was folding her in its cold embrace, but, just as those dark billows began rolling over her, they were turned to bright dashing waves of glory. She looked up and said, "How beautiful everything appears!"

A lady who was present said, "I do not see anything beautiful."

"No," replied the dying woman, "there is nothing in this house but dirt and rags, but I see things beautiful and lovely."

Her face then lit up with a happy look, and, as her countenance broke into a smile, her spirit took its flight to bright mansions of bliss. I stood and looked upon her lifeless form, with the peaceful expression on her face, and thought about the fact that death to the child of God is but the gate of heaven.

—Shaw, *Dying Testimonies of Saved and Unsaved*

# "My Peace Is Made with God!"

*Submitted by his daughter, Mrs. S. A. Slade, of Portland, New York, 1898*

My dear father, William H. Whitford, was seized with a severe hemorrhage of the lungs and died a few days later. He was a devoted Christian, and, as long as he was able to speak, he would greet us with a cheery, "Praise the Lord!" He had suffered from a complication of disorders that often caused him severe pain. When suffering, he would often go to God in prayer, secure relief, and get richly blessed in his soul.

One morning, his face was lit up with a holy light as he shouted, "Hallelujah! Glory to God!" A sister, who was in the next room, said that she, too, felt the power of the Holy Spirit and began rejoicing in God. Oh, how the Spirit would come upon us during those last days. Indeed, it was a heavenly place; the gloom was all taken away. It did not seem like dying.

Although father was eighty-two when he died, his mind was clear all the time, and he would think of everything needful to be done. His only desire to live was to help me, as we lived alone. But he also gave that to the Lord.

He talked about his funeral very calmly and selected the text: "*Mark the perfect man, and behold the upright: for the end of that man is peace*" (Psalm 37:37). He desired that the old hymns be sung. I asked him if he wanted flowers, to which he replied, "Oh, no. I want it very plain—clothed in righteousness."

He sang with us a short time before he went, and it was marvelous how his face glowed with joy while singing. "Hallelujah! Glory to God!" he shouted. Then, he clapped his hands and said, "If I could only get up, I feel I could leap and shout for joy. Peace, peace—my peace is made with God! I am filled with His love! Jesus alone heaves into sight!"

It seemed as though he could actually see heaven. His last words were, "Oh, bless the Lord! Praise the Lord!" Thus, he went sweetly to sleep, safe in the arms of Jesus.

—Shaw, *Dying Testimonies of Saved and Unsaved*

# "I Am as Much Lost as Though I Were in Hell Already!"

*Submitted by Mrs. H. A. Coon*

Another lady and I were asked to visit a neighbor who was sick and in terrible distress of soul. We went to his home and found the poor man pacing the floor and groaning. I said to him, "Mr. C—, we have come to help you, if that is your desire."

"I know it," he replied. "You are all right; but it is too late. I attended your meetings two years ago. The Spirit said to me, 'Hurry! Go to the altar! Plead with God for mercy!' I could scarcely sit on the seat. But I didn't. Then, I came to Marengo and was under deep conviction, but I would not yield. Finally, the Spirit left me, and I am as much lost as though I were in hell already!"

He struck his breast, saying, "I feel the fire is kindled here already. It is too late; I am going to hell—and my sons with me!"

He lived two more weeks. It was a place of darkness and devils until he died.

—Shaw, *Dying Testimonies of Saved and Unsaved*

John Myers

# "How Beautiful! How Beautiful!"

*Submitted by Rev. J. T. Leise*

I thought it might be to the glory of God to give you an account of my mother's death. She died July 28, 1888, in the township of Winnebago City, Minnesota. Approximately six months before her death, I had left home to enter the work of the Lord. At that time, and for years prior, mother had what we often called an up-and-down experience. On July 1, I got word to return home to see her die.

On my arrival, I found Mother very low but having a strong faith in God.

I said, "Mother, you have a better experience than you have ever had!"

"Yes, Johnnie," she said, "about three months ago I got what I have longed for for years."

Mother's disease was dropsy. With limbs swollen, she would suffer intensely, but her faith in Jesus never wavered. She would often speak of the glorious prospects in view. The morning she died, about four a.m., a sister and I were sitting by her bed fanning her when she opened her eyes and said, "Children, is this death? How beautiful! How beautiful!"

I said, "Mother, you will soon be at rest. It won't be long before you shall have crossed over and are home."

Mother never could sing to amount to anything, but, on this occasion, she sang an old hymn, as if inspired from heaven:

I long to be there
And His glories to share
And to lean on my Savior's breast.

About four hours later, we were around her bed having family worship when, without a struggle, she passed away to be forever with the Lord.

—Shaw, *Dying Testimonies of Saved and Unsaved*

# Charles V
## (1558)

*Holy Roman Emperor, King of Italy, King of Spain, and Lord of the Netherlands*

Born at Ghent in the year 1500, Charles V is said to have fought sixty battles, most of which were victorious. He obtained six triumphs, conquered four kingdoms, and added eight principalities to his dominions—an almost unparalleled instance of worldly prosperity and greatness of human glory.

But all this fruit of his ambition, and all the honors that attended him, could not yield true and solid satisfaction. While reflecting on the evils and miseries that he had occasioned, and being convinced of the emptiness of earthly magnificence, this great man became disgusted with all the splendor that surrounded him. He felt it both his duty and privilege to withdraw from it and desired to spend the rest of his days in spiritual retirement.

Accordingly, he set about to resign all his dominions to his brother and son, and, after an affectionate farewell to these and the retinue of princes and nobility who had respectfully attended him, he departed to a retreat in Spain, a vale of no great extent, watered by a small brook and surrounded by rising grounds covered with lofty trees.

As soon as he landed in Spain, he fell prostrate on the ground and kissed the earth, saying, "Naked came I out of my mother's womb, and naked I now return to thee, thou common mother of mankind."

In his humble retreat, the once great king now spent his time in spiritual communion with God and in innocent employments. In solitude and silence, he buried there his grandeur and ambition, together with all those vast projects, which, for nearly half a century, had alarmed and agitated Europe and filled every kingdom in it, by turns, with the terror of his arms and the dread of being subjected to his power.

Far from taking any part in the political transactions of the world, he restrained his curiosity even from any inquiry concerning them. He seemed to view the busy scene he had abandoned with an elevation and indifference of mind born of a thorough experience of its vanity, as well as the pleasing reflection of having disengaged himself from its cares and temptations.

The full proof of the happiness of those last years is seen in the short but comprehensive testimony this extraordinary man left to posterity: "I have tasted more satisfaction in my solitude in one day than in all the triumphs of my former reign. The sincere study, profession, and practice of the Christian religion have in them such joys and sweetness as are seldom found in courts and grandeur."

—Murray, *Power of Religion on the Mind*

# "Oh! Do You Hear the Music?"

*Submitted by Sadie A. Cryer of Rockford, Illinois*

May Wilcox of Marengo, Illinois, died when only twenty-one years of age. She was a self-sacrificing, devoted Christian. Shortly after conversion, she felt called of God to work for souls and began to give her life for others' sake. She proved faithful in her ministry and in every way was a worthy example of a child of God.

At the close of a series of meetings in Bradford, Illinois, May went home to recruit for the next battle but instead was stricken with typhoid fever. She lingered in its heat and suffering a little over a month. Then, Jesus came and took her to Himself.

Once during her sickness, her mother came in, but the dying girl was unconscious of all around and failed to recognize her. Her mother said, "May, do you know Jesus?"

"Jesus? Oh, yes, I know Jesus!"

The mentioning of His name brought consciousness to May. She well knew that name.

Shortly before she passed away, the loved ones who were then outside of the ark of safety were called to her bedside. She tried to exhort them to prepare to meet God, but her tongue was too swollen, and they could not understand. However, the Lord did enable May to tell, in a more elegant way than words, of the glories that filled her soul in that wonderful hour, for she suddenly threw up her arms and exclaimed, "Oh! Do you hear the music?"

The unsaved ones standing around her bed saw the light that came from heaven into that little room, and they felt its divine influence. God had spoken!

Her soul then took its flight, and the career of one triumphant in life, and, now, also in death, was ended.

—Shaw, *Dying Testimonies of Saved and Unsaved*

# "Madge Is Dead, and David Is Crazy!"

*Submitted by Rev. F. A. Ames*

It was the spring of 1891, and Rev. C. B. Ebey was holding special church services in Colgrove, California. Among others, two young ladies and their brother were awakened to their need of Christ. However, they held back from making the decision.

The younger of the two girls was a bright, healthy girl of fourteen named Madge. One day, Reverend Ebey said to her, "Madge, I believe this meeting is being held for you."

The girl sensed these words were from God and, after thinking it over, decided she must surely give her heart to God. Her brother, David, then intervened. He dearly loved her, and, knowing that if she became a Christian, their worldly pleasures together would end, he persuaded her to wait a few years. "Then," he insisted, "we'll both get saved." Thus, they agreed and said to the Holy Spirit, "Wait until a more convenient season."

A few weeks later, Reverend Ebey received the startling message that Madge was dead and that he should come to her home immediately. He went as quickly as he could and was met at the door by the distraught mother.

"Oh, Brother Ebey," she sobbed, "you have come to a sad home. Madge is dead, and David is crazy!"

Gradually, he unraveled the story from the weeping woman. When the doctor had said that Madge could not possibly live, David went wild and rushed to her bedside. There he knelt and prayed, as only a sinner could, that God might save his sister's soul. He then urged Madge to pray, but she was too sick to make any effort and died without leaving any evidence of salvation.

The strain of realizing that his beloved sister was dying without Christ, and that he was the cause of it, was too much for the young man. His reason gave way.

—Shaw, *Dying Testimonies of Saved and Unsaved*

# The Artist and the Gypsy Girl

Many years ago, in the old city of Dusseldorf in northwest Germany, there lived an artist by the name of Stenburg. A Roman Catholic, he had been taught doctrine and ceremony but knew nothing of Christ as his own Savior from the guilt and power of sin. He had been engaged to paint a great picture of the crucifixion, and this he was doing, not from any real love of Christ or faith in Him, but simply for money and fame.

One beautiful spring morning, Stenburg was seeking recreation in the forest near Dusseldorf when he came upon a Gypsy girl named Pepita plaiting straw baskets. She was unusually beautiful, and Stenburg determined to engage her as model for his painting of a Spanish dancing girl. After some bargaining, she at last agreed to come to his studio three times each week.

At the appointed hour, Pepita arrived. As her great eyes roved around the studio, she was full of wonder; then, the large picture of the crucifixion caught her eye. Gazing at it intently and pointing to the figure on the cross in the center, she asked, in an awed voice, "Who is that?"

"The Christ," answered Stenburg, carelessly.

"What is being done to Him?"

"They are crucifying Him."

"Who are those about Him with the bad faces?"

"Now, look here," said the artist, "I cannot talk. You have nothing to do but stand as I tell you."

The girl dared not speak again, but she continued to gaze. Every time she came to the studio, the fascination of the painting grew on her. Finally, she ventured to ask another question.

"Why did they crucify Him? Was He bad—very bad?"

"No," the artist replied, "very good."

That was all she learned at that interview, but it added a little to her knowledge of that wonderful scene.

At last, seeing she was so anxious to know the meaning of the painting, Stenburg said, "Listen, I will tell you once and for all. Then ask no more questions!"

So, he told her the story of the cross—new to Pepita, though so old to the artist that it had ceased to touch him. He could paint that dying agony without the quiver of a nerve. The thought of it wrung the Gypsy's heart. Tears filled her eyes.

Pepita's last visit to the studio had come. She stood before the great painting, loath to leave it.

"Come," said the artist, "here is your money, and a gold piece over."

"Thanks, Master," she murmured. Then, again turning to the painting, she said: "You must love Him very much, since He has done all that for you—do you not?"

Stenburg could not answer.

Pepita went back to her people, but God's Spirit sent the Gypsy girl's words home to the artist's heart. He could not forget them. "All that for you" rang in his ears. He became restless and sad. He knew he did not love the crucified One.

Sometime later, Stenburg was impressed to follow a few poor people who gathered to hear the Bible read. There, for the first time, he met those who had a living faith. Hearing the simple gospel message, he was made to realize why Christ had hung on the cross for sinners. He saw that he was a sinner and, therefore, that Christ was there for him, bearing his sins.

He began to know the love of Christ and soon could say, "He loved me and gave Himself for me."

At once, he longed to make that wondrous love known to others. But how could he do it? Suddenly, it flashed upon him: he could paint. His brush could spell out the love of Christ! Praying for God's help, he resumed his work on the crucifixion painting as never before. When finished, the work was placed among other paintings in the famous gallery of Dusseldorf. Underneath, the artist had placed these words: "All this I did for thee; what hast thou done for Me?"

Eternity alone will tell how many have been led to Christ by those words and that painting.

One day, Stenburg saw a poorly dressed girl weeping bitterly as she stood by the painting. It was Pepita.

"Oh, Master, if He had but loved me so," she cried.

Then, the artist told her how He did die for her, poor Gypsy girl though she was, as much as for the rich and great. He did not weary now of answering all her eager questions. He was as anxious to tell as she was to hear of the love of Christ.

As Pepita listened, she received, and the age-old miracle of spiritual new birth took place. She went from that room a new creature in God's wonderful love. Thus, the Lord used Pepita's words to bring the artist to Himself and then used the artist's words to reveal Himself to her.

Months afterward, Stenburg was called by a dark-looking stranger to visit a dying person. He followed his guide through the streets and into the country, and then beyond, into the deep forest. At last, they came to a few poor tents in a sheltered spot. In one of these, he found Pepita. She was dying in poverty, but she was happy in the precious love of Christ.

He watched her die while she praised her Savior for His love, knowing that He had taken away all her sins and that she was going into His blessed presence to be forever with Him.

Long after this, when the artist, too, had gone to be with the Lord, a wealthy young nobleman found his way into that gallery in Dusseldorf. As he gazed upon the painting and the words beneath it, God spoke to his heart, there and then.

Hours later, when the guard came to close the gallery for the day, the young man was still on his knees in tears before that scene.

That young man was the famous Count Zinzendorf, who from that day became an earnest Christian and later became the father of the renowned Moravian missions, by means of which God led thousands of men and women in many lands to Himself.

# "I'm Halfway Between Two Worlds"

*Submitted by Arline Sexauer of Northbridge, California*

When my mother, Eleanor Herrick, died of cancer in December 1964, it was a time of joy and triumph instead of sadness and defeat. Mother was a born-again Christian of deep faith.

In her final illness, she spent about two weeks in the hospital. My brother, Don, and I were with her every day. The last three days, she started slipping into a coma and spoke little to us.

The day before she died, she said, "Oh, Arline, I feel as though I am cradled in love—from this side and the next."

The next day, she spoke her last words. When I entered her room, the patient in the bed next to hers called me over and asked, "Who is Margaret? Your mother has been talking to Margaret all morning." I told her that Margaret was my mother's sister who had died years ago.

Then, I went to Mother's side, took her hand, and told her who I was. She spoke her last words in this world: "Oh, Arline, it's so strange here. I'm in a 'never-never land.' I'm halfway between two worlds. Ma and Pa are here, and I can see them, but I can't see you anymore."

# Sir Francis Newport (1708)

Sir Francis Newport was taught the great truths of the gospel in his early life, and, when he was yet a young man, it was hoped that he would become a tribute and a blessing to his family, as well as his nation. However, the result was far different. He fell into company that corrupted his principles and morals, and he became an avowed infidel. The life of dissipation that followed soon brought on a disease that was incurable.

When he realized that he was doomed to die, he threw himself on his bed and, after a brief pause, exclaimed, "Whence this war in my heart? What argument is there now to assist me against matters of fact? Do I assert that there is no hell, while I feel one in my own bosom? Am I certain there is no retribution after death, when I feel present judgment? Do I affirm my soul to be as mortal as my body, when this languishes, and the soul is vigorous as ever? Oh, that someone would restore to me that ancient gourd of piety and innocence! Wretch that I am, where shall I flee from this breast? What will become of me?"

An infidel companion tried to dispel his thoughts, but Newport answered, "That there is a God, I know, because I continually feel the effects of His wrath. That there is a hell, I am equally certain, having received an earnest of my inheritance there already in my breast. That there is a natural conscience, I now feel with horror and amazement, being continually upbraided by it with my impieties and all my iniquities brought to my remembrance."

To the dismay of his former friend, he continued, "Why God has marked me out for an example of His vengeance rather than you, or anyone of my acquaintance, I presume, is because I have been more religiously educated, and thus have done greater despite to the Spirit of grace. Oh, that I were to lie upon the fire that never is quenched a thousand years to purchase the favor of God. But it is a fruitless wish. Millions of millions of years will bring me no nearer to the end of my torments than one poor hour. Oh, eternity, eternity! Who can discover the abyss of eternity? Who can paraphrase upon these words: 'forever and ever'?"

When some of his friends thought him insane, he said, "You imagine me to be melancholy or distracted. I wish I were either; but it is part of my awful judgment that I am not. No, my apprehension of persons and things is more quick and vigorous than it was when I was in perfect health—and it is my curse, because I am thus more sensible of my condition.

"Would you be informed why I am become a skeleton in three or four days? It is because I have despised my Maker and denied my Redeemer. I joined myself to the atheist and profane and continued this course, in spite of many convictions, till my iniquity was ripe for vengeance. The just judgment of God overtook me when my security was the greatest and the checks of my conscience were the least."

As his mental distress and bodily disease were hurrying him into eternity, he was asked if he wanted prayer offered on his behalf. Turning his face away, he exclaimed, "Tigers and monsters! Are you also become devils to torment me? Would you give me prospect of heaven to make my hell more intolerable?"

Soon after this, his voice failed, and, uttering a groan of inexpressible horror, he cried out, "Oh, the insufferable pangs of hell!"—and was gone.

—Shaw, *Dying Testimonies of Saved and Unsaved*

# "I Saw the Spiritual World"

*Submitted by George Godkin of Geo. Godkin and Sons Contractors, Ltd., of Turner Valley, Alberta, Canada*

Have you ever given thought to the subject of death? What transpires when we lose sight of the known and enter the unknown? I never gave this subject much thought until 1948, when a serious event in my life jolted me into some serious thinking.

Before I relate my unusual experience, let me state that I thought I was living an interesting and sensational life. But, for me, real life began after this event.

In midwinter, a natural gas explosion and fire wrecked our home. The gas line broke, and the house became an inferno—a high-pressure ball of fire. At the time, I was in the basement. To get outside, I had to run through the flames. In the frozen snow stood my wife with one of our children that she had rescued.

"Maureen is in the bedroom," she cried.

The heat was insufferable, but I went back in. Searing flames licked at me. I felt my way through the fire with our six-week-old baby in my arms. After escaping, I was rushed to the hospital with third-degree burns covering 65 percent of my body. At that time, medical statistics maintained that the human body could not survive with more than 40 percent of the body burned.

So far as man's philosophy knows, life's journey ends in blackest night. What happened to me next may appear to be more fantasy than reality. I traveled into that land beyond death—and returned. Let me relate some things to you, as I saw them.

One of the first things the conscious soul is aware of in the "resurrection world" is a sense of weightlessness as the soul leaves the physical body. It is the earthly body that gives the soul that heavy feeling that comes with gravity. It is quite an experience to look back at your physical body lying on a hospital bed. As I got over the shock of separation from my earthly body and realized that I was now in the spiritual world, I was amazed at the vast difference between these two dimensions.

First was the clear separation of light and darkness. The light was soft, gentle, and constant, whereas the darkness had depth and weight and seemed depressing. There seemed to be no time factor in the spiritual world; also, no sense of distance or space as we know it here. But there were rules and regulations with areas that are reserved for classified beings.

It seems to be a popular assumption that in the world beyond death, people flit around like butterflies, going wherever they want and doing as they please. Nothing could be further from the truth. There is a system of order in the resurrection world. There are two distinct places of abode, with a great gulf of separation between them. There is a power there that prohibits the individual soul from traveling from one shore to the other. I stood amazed when I noticed that all classes of people were going to both sides—rich and poor, good and bad, including the vilest of humanity. Some entered the place of marvelous peace and contentment, while others went into utter darkness, where the agony is something that has never been experienced here on earth.

I wondered why the stream of humanity divided. What qualification gave some permission to enter the place of contentment while others were banished to darkness?

After I returned to this earthly body, the Spirit of God led me to the Bible, which revealed to me that Christ is the only entrance into the area of eternal pleasure after the death of your mortal body. Only since I have accepted Christ as my own personal Savior do I have the assurance of peace and contentment that leads to eternal life.

# Sir John Mason (1566)

A strong testimony to the importance of spiritual life is given by Sir John Mason, who, though but sixty-three at his death, had flourished in the reigns of four sovereigns—Henry VIII, Edward VI, Mary, and Elizabeth. He had been privy-counselor to them all and was an attentive observer of the various revolutions and vicissitudes of those times.

Toward his latter end, being on his deathbed, he spoke thus to those about him: "I have lived to see five sovereigns and have been privy-counselor to four of them. I have seen the most remarkable things in foreign parts and have been present at most state transactions for the last thirty years. I have learned from this experience of so many years that seriousness is the greatest wisdom, temperance the best physic, and a good conscience the best estate. And, were I to live again, I would change the court for a cloister, my privy-counselor's bustle for a hermit's retirement, and the whole life I have lived in the palace for an hour's enjoyment of God in the chapel. All things now forsake me except my God, my duty, and my prayers."

From the regret expressed by Sir John Mason, it appears that his error consisted not in having served his king and country in the eminent stations in which he had been placed but in having suffered his mind to be so much occupied with business as to make him neglect, in some degree, the proper seasons of spiritual retirement and the prime duties which he owed to his Creator.

—Murray, *Power of Religion on the Mind*

# "It Is Jesus, Father, Who Has Come to Take Me"

A little girl, Naglie, was a resident of Jerusalem. Her mother, too, was a Christian and had learned to love Jesus in Miss Arnott's school in Jaffa.

Just before Naglie died, she said, "It is Jesus, Father, who has come to take me. There He is at the foot of my bed; He calls me to come."

—Gottschall, *Selections from Testimonies and Dying Words*

# Sent Back from Heaven for Seven Years

If Jewel Rose could lean down over the battlements of heaven and call back a message to his fellow workers here on earth, surely he would lift his hand, turn on that beaming smile of his, and shout, "Have faith! Never fear! My God can do anything!"

And, standing happily beside him, his beloved wife, Florence, would smile her complete agreement—for God, in His loving kindness, called them both home on February 16, 1968.

During the years since Jewel's miraculous healing, these two people have ministered side by side in the gospel field, and it was so fitting that they should pass through the gates together.

In 1953, Mr. Rose was elected to the International Board of Directors of the Full Gospel Business Men's Fellowship International, and from 1958 to 1967, he also served as International Secretary-Treasurer. However, in 1967, he felt it necessary to resign all official positions and give his full time to preaching the gospel. In fact, Jewel and Florence were on their way to another gospel meeting when God called them home.

A few months ago, Jewel had remarked that he felt that he would be "going home soon." His wife said, "Then, I want to go, too." He replied, "Well, Mama, the Lord can take care of that."

"I visited the beautiful gate," Mr. Rose testified. "I wanted to go in then, but the Lord sent me back to preach the gospel and to testify to His glory." Seven years prior, in answer to the prayers of several men from his church, God had brought Jewel back to life after he had been given up on as dead by his doctors. After this miraculous healing, he felt that the Lord impressed upon him that he would have seven more years, and, thus, he began to anticipate the end as the seven years drew to a close.

One week before the end, with no outward reason whatever, he told Mr. Cecil Poole, District Superintendent of the Pentecostal Church of God, that he felt his time was up. Florence said that she had always wanted for them to go together and that the reason God had brought him back to life was partly for this reason, as well as to continue in ministry.

On February 16, these two precious lovers were together, arm in arm, as they drove to meet a preaching engagement. Mr. Rose must have mistakenly turned off the highway at the wrong road before deciding to back up in order to get back on the main road. Another car struck them from the rear.

A highway patrolman said he found them dead, still sitting arm in arm. Neither of them seemed to have had a scratch on them, though the car was completely demolished.

This time, there would be no returning to life, at least not until Jesus returns, for Jewel and Florence Rose have gone home, so abundantly ready, and with their arms filled with sheaves.

An empty chair at the council table; the voice of a mighty prayer warrior silenced; the absence of his never-flagging spiritual strength in helping to carry the burden of the Lord's work. All these things are felt by the Fellowship with a sense of great loss. Yet the loss is compensated by our last memory of Jewel, standing on a convention platform, his head thrown back as though looking upward toward heaven, his voice booming out in the song:

O that will be glory for me,
Glory for me, glory for me,
When by His grace I shall look on His face,
That will be glory, be glory for me![23]

—Adapted from *Full Gospel Business Men's Voice,* March 1968

# Patrick Hamilton
# (1528)

*Scottish Reformer and Martyr*

On the first of March, 1528, some eight years before Tyndale was betrayed and executed, Archbishop Beaton condemned Patrick Hamilton to be burned because he advocated the doctrines of the Reformation.

The principal accusations were that he taught it was proper for the poor people to read God's Word and that it was useless to offer masses for the souls of the dead. Hamilton admitted the truth of these charges and boldly defended his doctrines. He was, therefore, quickly condemned, and, to avoid any possibility of his rescue by influential friends, in but a few hours, the stake was prepared before the gate of St. Salvador College.

When the martyr was brought forth, he removed his outer garments and gave them to his servant, saying, "These will not profit me in the fire, but they will profit thee. Hereafter, thou canst have no profit from me except the example of

23. Charles H. Gabriel, "O That Will Be Glory," 1900.

my death, which I pray thee keep in memory; for, though bitter to the flesh and fearful before man, it is the door of eternal life, which none will attain who denies Christ Jesus before this ungodly generation."

His agony was prolonged by a slow fire, so that his execution lasted some six hours. But, through it all, he manifested true heroism and unshaken faith. His last words were, "How long, O Lord, shall darkness brood over this realm? How long wilt Thou suffer this tyranny of man? Lord Jesus, receive my spirit!"

Thus, in the bloom of early manhood died Scotland's first Reformation martyr, whose death was not in vain. A Romanist afterward said, "The smoke of Patrick Hamilton infected all it blew upon."

That was true, for though his mouth was closed, the story of his death was repeated by a thousand tongues. It emboldened others to seek a martyr's crown and stirred up many more to defend the truths for which he died and to repudiate the hierarchy which found it necessary to defend itself by such means.

"Humanly speaking," wrote James Hardy in *Champions of the Reformation* (1869), "could there have been found a fitter apostle for ignorant, benighted Scotland than this eloquent, fervent, pious man? Endowed with all those gifts that sway the heads of the masses—a zealous and pious laborer, in season and out of season—what herculean labors might he have accomplished! What signal triumphs might he have achieved! So men may reason, but God judged otherwise. A short trial, a brief essay on the work he loved and longed for was permitted to him, and then, the goodly vessel, still in sight of land, was broken in pieces."

—Shaw, *Dying Testimonies of Saved and Unsaved*

# "Praise Him, All of You!"

*Submitted by Mrs. V. E. Markin of Litchfield, Kentucky*

Ethel was a bright, beautiful young girl with whom we were acquainted. Her mother was a Christian who endeavored to impress upon her daughter's mind the importance of being born again—not of water, but of the Holy Spirit. Through the influence of roommates and associates while attending boarding school, Ethel had been led to believe that simply making a public confession of faith in Christ and the sacrament of baptism by immersion were all that was needed for salvation.

Ethel's mother knew from past experience that God was faithful, so, by persistent faith and daily prayer, she called upon Him to show Ethel the error of resting on church ordinances for spiritual safety. She patiently pointed out that only the blood of Christ and a saving faith in its atoning merits could secure to her soul eternal life and a home in heaven.

One day, after much prayer, the mother was greatly comforted by receiving the assurance of the Holy Spirit that God would eventually turn Ethel from the error of building her hopes on a foundation of sand.

Not long after this, although only twenty-two, Ethel knew that she stood with the billows of death rolling very near her feet. She then began to realize that water baptism would not avail to rescue her soul from the perils of sin and the coming judgment. "Man's extremity is ever God's opportunity," and the Holy Spirit began to convince her of her need of Jesus as a personal Savior.

The conflict of her soul with doubts and fears was short but severe. Faith, at length, triumphed. Only five days before her death, Ethel had been speechless for hours. Then, her mother, who was near her couch, heard Ethel say, with great effort, "Whosoever...will...may come."

Then, the saving power of the Holy Spirit fell upon her heart, and, as a bright smile overspread her beautiful young face, she exclaimed, "Praise Him, all of you! Praise Him!" Those were Ethel's last words on earth.

—Shaw, *Dying Testimonies of Saved and Unsaved*

# Lady Hope's Visit with Charles Darwin

It may surprise many students of evolution to learn that in the closing days of his life, Charles Darwin returned to his faith in the Bible. The following account is told by Lady Hope of Northfield, England, a wonderful Christian woman who was often at his bedside before he died:

> It was one of those glorious autumn afternoons, which we sometimes enjoy in England, when I was asked to go in and sit with the well-known professor Charles Darwin. He was almost bedridden for some months before he died. I used to feel when I saw him that his fine presence would make a grand picture for our Royal Academy, but never did I think so more strongly than on this particular occasion.
>
> He was sitting up in bed, wearing a soft embroidered dressing gown of rather a rich purple shade.
>
> Propped up by pillows, he was gazing out on a far-stretching scene of woods and cornfields, which glowed in the light of one of those marvelous sunsets which are the beauty of Kent and Surrey. His noble forehead and fine features seemed to be lit up with pleasure as I entered the room.
>
> He waved his hand toward the window as he pointed out the scene beyond, while in the other hand he held an open Bible, which he was always studying.
>
> "What are you reading now?" I asked, as I seated myself beside his bedside.
>
> "Hebrews!" he answered. "Still Hebrews. 'The Royal Book,' I call it. Isn't it grand?"
>
> Then, placing his finger on certain passages, he commented on them. I made some allusions to the strong opinions expressed by many persons

on the history of the creation and its grandeur and then their treatment of the earlier chapters of the book of Genesis.

He seemed greatly distressed; his fingers twitched nervously, and a look of agony came over his face, as he said, "I was a young man with unformed ideas. I threw out queries, suggestions, wondering all the time over everything, and, to my astonishment, the ideas took like wildfire. People made a religion of them."

Then, he paused, and, after a few more sentences on "the holiness of God" and "the grandeur of this book," he said, "I have a summer house in the garden, which holds about thirty people. It is over there." He pointed through the open window. "I want you very much to speak there. I know you read the Bible in the villages. Tomorrow afternoon, I should like the servants on the place, some tenants, and a few of the neighbors to gather there. Will you speak to them?"

"What shall I speak about?" I asked.

"Christ Jesus!" he replied in a clear, emphatic voice, adding, in a lower tone, "and His salvation. Is not that the best theme? And then, I want you to sing some hymns with them. You lead on your small instrument, do you not?" The wonderful look of brightness and animation on his face as he said this I shall never forget, for he added, "If you take the meeting at three o'clock, this window will be open, and you will know that I am joining in with the singing."

How I wished I could have made a picture of the fine old man and his beautiful surroundings on that memorable day!

—From the *Watchman-Examiner,* August 1915

# "Ma, I Shall Be the First of Our Family Over Yonder"

*Submitted by Rev. G. R. Vanhorne*

Asa Hart Alling, eldest son of Rev. J. H. and Jennie Alling, died April 19, 1881, in Chicago at the age of fourteen. He was converted and united with the church when eleven. While most boys were devoting their spare time to fun and sport, he applied himself to works of love. Numerous aged and infirm people living near Simpson Church will bear record to the good deeds by his youthful hands. In the public school, he took high rank and led his classmates. For his years, he was well advanced.

On Friday, April 15, he complained of being ill but insisted on going to school. He soon returned in distress, however, and went to bed, never to leave it. He had been stricken with cerebrospinal meningitis.

At times, he suffered great agony, but, through it all, he proved himself a hero and a Christian conqueror. He realized that his sickness was fatal and talked about death with composure. He put his arms about his mother's neck and, gently drawing her face close to his own, said, "Ma, I shall be the first of our family over yonder, but I will stand on the shore and wait for you all to come."

He then requested his mother to sing the hymn "Pull for the Shore." She, being completely overcome with grief, could not sing. He said, "Never mind, Ma; you will sing it after I am gone, won't you?"

To a Christian lady who came to see him, he said, "Will you sing for me? Sing 'Hold the Fort'!" She sang it. "Now sing 'Hallelujah! 'Tis Done.'" He fully realized that the work of his salvation was done and that he was "holding the fort" until he should be called up higher.

He bestowed his treasures upon his brother and sisters. He gave his Bible to his brother, Treat, and, as he did so, said to his father, "Pa, tell Aunty that I died a Christian." Aunty had been the one who had given Asa his Bible.

His last hours of consciousness were rapidly closing. He remarked, "Ma, I shall not live till morning; I am so tired and want to go to sleep. If I do not wake up, good-bye—good-bye all!"

A short time afterward, he fell asleep in Jesus. *"He was not; for God took him"* (Genesis 5:24).

He had reached the shores of eternal life for which he had pulled so earnestly and with success. His funeral was attended by a large concourse of people who thronged the church. We all felt as if we had lost a treasure and heaven had gained a jewel.

—Shaw, *Dying Testimonies of Saved and Unsaved*

# John Wesley
# (1791)

This great servant of Christ went to heaven on March 2, 1791, in the eighty-eighth year of his life, after preaching the gospel for sixty-five years.

Shortly before his death, Mr. Wesley said, "I will get up."

While they arranged his clothes, he broke out singing in a manner which astonished all about him:

I'll praise my Maker while I've breath;
And when my voice is lost in death,
Praise shall employ my nobler powers.
My days of praise shall ne'er be past,
While life, and thought, and being last,
Or immortality endures.

Happy the man whose hopes rely
On Israel's God, who made the sky
And earth and seas, with all their train;

Whose truth forever stands secure,
He saves th'oppressed and feeds the poor,
For none shall find God's promise vain.[24]

Once more seated in his chair, in a weak voice, he said, "Speak, Lord, to all our hearts, and let them know that Thou loosest tongues."

Then, he again sang a couple of lines:

To Father, Son, and Holy Ghost,
Who sweetly all agree....

Here, his voice failed, but, after resting a little, he called to those who were with him to "pray and praise." He took each by the hand and, after affectionately saluting them, bade them farewell.

After attempting to say something that they could not understand, he paused a little, and then, with all his remaining strength, he said, "The best of all is God is with us!"

And again, lifting his hand, he repeated the same words in holy triumph: "The best of all is God is with us!"

Most of the following night, he repeatedly tried to repeat the hymn he had sung but could only say, "I'll praise, I'll praise."

On Wednesday morning, the end was near. Joseph Bradford prayed with him about ten o'clock in the morning, while eleven friends knelt around the bed.

"Farewell," said the dying man—the last word he spoke. Without a groan or a sigh, he passed away. His friends quietly rose and, while standing around his bed, sang:

Waiting to receive thy spirit,
Lo, the Savior stands above,
Shews the purchase of His merit,
Reaches out the crown of love![25]

—Edith C. Kenyon, *The Centenary Life of John Wesley* (1890)

24. Isaac Watts, "I'll Praise My Maker While I've Breath," 1719.
25. Charles Wesley, "The Departing Saint," 1749.

# Miracle Words on a Vietnamese Battlefield

George was different. Some of the other marines professed Christianity, but George lived it. His sergeant, John McElhannon, a Navajo Indian, did not claim to believe anything. However, he saw in George a man to be respected and admired, and they soon became good friends.

One day, their company was attacked during a battle with the Viet Cong, and George was critically wounded. John rushed to where the stricken George lay and encouraged him, "You're going to be all right; take it easy and save your strength."

In his weakened condition, George could say only a few words: "John, you need God." But he said them in the Navajo language! The young marine, enabled by the Holy Spirit, was employing the gift of tongues in the more unusual expression of the gift, one which enables the believer to speak in a known language that is unknown to him. (See Mark 16:17–18; 1 Corinthians 12:7–11; Acts 2:4–6.)

Sgt. McElhannon was astounded. He had often tried to teach George words and phrases in his native tongue, but to no avail. Now, in flawless Navajo, came these startling words, which proved to be the last George would ever speak.

Afterward, John McElhannon also was struck down in battle and had to return to the U.S. to recuperate. As he lay in the hospital, the dying words of his fallen comrade went through his mind, and he couldn't forget them: "John, you need God." He determined that he must find George's God.

After a futile visit to at least one church in San Francisco, John went to Fresno, California, to visit his mother. There, he again took up his quest to find the God whom George had known and loved so ardently. He tried one church but found nothing to satisfy the longing in his heart. Then, just as he was planning to leave the city, he decided to try once more. As he picked up the phone book to scan its pages, the name Bethel Temple attracted his attention. A call to the pastor led to a Saturday night young people's meeting in a home.

It took only a few moments in the warmth and love of that home meeting to convince John that these young people knew George's God. He became so excited that, at first, the group became alarmed. As he unburdened his heart, however, and told them about George, suspicion turned to joy. With their eager prayers and help, the young ex-soldier soon put his faith in Jesus Christ and found George's God to be his own God. The quest had ended, giving 1st Lieutenant John McElhannon of the U.S. Marines his own inspiring testimony.

—Adapted from original sources by the editor

# Jesus Christ

The following testimony is composed of selected passages from the gospels of Matthew and John in the New Testament.

The story climaxes at the close of Jesus' three years of ministry, when He was thirty-three years of age:

> *And Jesus going up to Jerusalem took the twelve disciples apart in the way, and said unto them, Behold, we go up to Jerusalem; and the Son of man shall be betrayed unto the chief priests and unto the scribes, and they shall condemn him to death, and shall deliver him to the Gentiles to mock, and to scourge, and to crucify him: and the third day he shall rise again.*
>
> (Matthew 20:17–20)

> *Jesus knew that his hour was come that he should depart out of this world unto the Father.* (John 13:1)

Therefore, after reaching Jerusalem, and while eating the Passover Supper with the disciples,

> *He took the cup, and gave thanks, and gave it to them, saying, Drink ye all of it; for this is my blood of the new testament, which is shed for many for the remission of sins.* (Matthew 26:27–28)

Anxiety filled the hearts of the disciples. Jesus knew this, and He said to them,

> *I go and prepare a place for you, I will come again, and receive you unto myself; that where I am, there ye may be also....Peace I leave with you, my peace I give unto you....Let not your heart be troubled, neither let it be afraid.*
> (John 14:3, 27)

> *These words spake Jesus, and lifted up his eyes to heaven, and said, Father, the hour is come; glorify thy Son, that thy Son also may glorify thee....I have glorified thee on the earth: I have finished the work which thou gavest me to do. And now, O Father, glorify thou me with thine own self with the glory which I had with thee before the world was....O righteous Father, the world hath not known thee: but I have known thee, and these have known that thou hast sent me. And I have declared unto them thy name, and will declare it: that the love wherewith thou hast loved me may be in them, and I in them.*
> (John 17:1, 4–5, 25–26)

After He was betrayed and the soldiers took Him, one of the disciples drew a sword and started to defend Him. Jesus at once restrained the young man, saying,

> *Put up again thy sword into his place: for all they that take the sword shall perish with the sword. Thinkest thou that I cannot now pray to my Father, and he shall presently give me more than twelve legions of angels? But how then shall the scriptures be fulfilled...?* (Matthew 26:52–54)

Jesus was arraigned before Pontius Pilate, the Roman governor.

Pilate asked Him, *"Art thou the King of the Jews?"* (John 18:33).

> *Jesus answered, My kingdom is not of this world: if my kingdom were of this world, then would my servants fight, that I should not be delivered to the Jews: but now is my kingdom not from hence. Pilate therefore said unto him, Art thou a king then? Jesus answered, Thou sayest that I am a king. To this end was I born, and for this cause came I into the world, that I should bear witness unto the truth. Every one that is of the truth heareth my voice.*
> (John 18:36–37)

Pilate then attempted to dismiss the charges against Jesus, saying, *"I find in him no fault at all"* (John 18:38). The Jews, however, were insistent: *"By our law he ought to die, because he made himself the Son of God"* (John 19:7).

When the governor heard this charge, he became disturbed and returned to the judgment hall.

> [Pilate] *went again into the judgment hall, and saith unto Jesus, Whence art thou? But Jesus gave him no answer. Then saith Pilate unto him, Speakest thou not unto me? knowest thou not that I have power to crucify thee, and have power to release thee? Jesus answered, Thou couldest have no power at all against me, except it were given thee from above.* (John 19:9–11)

After this, Pilate determined to release Jesus, but the Jews brought political pressure to bear, until Pilate was finally forced to order His execution.

As Jesus hung on the cross, He said little, aside from committing His mother to one of the disciples for personal care and promising one of the dying thieves who was crucified with Him that they would be in paradise together.

After several hours, *"Jesus cried with a loud voice, saying,...My God, my God, why hast thou forsaken me?"* (Matthew 27:46).

*"After this, Jesus knowing that all things were now accomplished..."* (John 19:28). *"Jesus, when he had cried again with a loud voice, yielded up the ghost"* (Matthew 27:50).

The declaration that Jesus *"yielded up the ghost"* sets His death apart from those of other men. Jesus died of His own volition when He could say of His sufferings as a sacrifice for sin in our stead, *"It is finished."* This is in accordance with what He had said several months before the crucifixion:

> *I lay down my life, that I might take it again. No man taketh it from me, but I lay it down of myself. I have power to lay it down, and I have power to take it again.* (John 10:17–18)

# I Shall Not Doubt Immortality

To every created thing, God has given a tongue that proclaims a resurrection. If the Father deigns to touch with divine power the cold and pulseless heart of the buried acorn and make it burst forth from its prison walls, will He leave neglected in the earth the soul of man, made in the image of his Creator? If He stoops to give the rose bush, whose withered blossoms float upon the autumn breeze, the sweet assurance of another springtime, will He refuse the word of hope to the sons of men when the frost of another winter comes? If matter, mute and inanimate, though changed by the force of nature into a multitude of forms, can never die, will the spirit of man suffer annihilation when it has paid a brief visit, like a royal guest, to the tenement of clay? No. I am as sure that there is another life as I am that I live today.

In Cairo, I secured a few grains of wheat that had slumbered for more than three thousand years in an Egyptian tomb. As I looked at them, this thought came into my mind: *If one of those grains had been planted upon the banks of the Nile the year after it grew, and all its lineal descendants planted and replanted from that time until now, its progeny would today be sufficiently numerous to feed the seething millions of the world.*

A grain of wheat has the power to discard its body and, from earth and air, fashion a new body so much like the old one that we cannot tell one from the other. If this invisible germ of life in the grain of wheat can thus pass unimpaired through three thousand resurrections, I shall not doubt that my soul has the power to clothe itself with a new body, suited to its new existence, when this earthly frame has crumbled into dust.

—William Jennings Bryan

# A Prayer of Salvation

The Bible tells us that we have *all* sinned and fall short of God's glory. (See Romans 3:23.) Scripture also tells that *"the wages of sin is death; but the gift of God is eternal life through Jesus Christ our Lord"* (Romans 6:23).

Thankfully, God loved us so much that He gave His only Son, Jesus, to die on the cross for us, so that we could be forgiven our sins. *"For God so loved the world, that he gave his only begotten Son, that whosoever believeth in him should not perish, but have everlasting life"* (John 3:16).

For us to accept this incredible gift of eternal salvation, we simply have to follow the steps outlined for us in Romans 10:9–10:

> *If thou shalt confess with thy mouth the Lord Jesus, and shalt believe in thine heart that God hath raised him from the dead, thou shalt be saved. For with the heart man believeth unto righteousness; and with the mouth confession is made unto salvation.*

First, we must confess with our mouths that we are sinners and that Jesus is Lord. Second, we must believe in our hearts that Jesus is the Son of God, and that God raised Him from the dead.

You can make this confession today and ensure your place in the heavenly family of God by saying this simple prayer:

> Dear Jesus, I believe that You are the Son of God and that You died on the cross for me and rose again so that I can be forgiven of my sins. I confess to You this day that I am a sinner. Please forgive me of my sins and come into my heart right now as my Lord and Savior. Amen.

If you prayed that prayer, you have made the most important decision you will ever make. Welcome to the family of God. Now, find a Bible-believing church and tell as many people as you can that you are now a Christian, bound for heaven and rescued from hell.

# About the Author

Dr. John Myers was raised in Lawrence, Kansas, a small "Jayhawker" town sitting in the shadow of Kansas University. After high school and three years in the army, "Dr. John's" undergraduate studies were quite diverse: basics at Bob Jones University, engineering at the University of Wisconsin, and three years of Bible study at Prairie Bible Institute in Alberta, Canada. After that, Dr. Myers earned a doctorate in Chiropractic at Palmer Chiropractic College in Davenport, Iowa.

After graduation and an extensive background in several areas of natural, nontoxic healing, Dr. Myers focused his research in the field of medical electronics. He has developed the DHSWT program (Dual-Harmonic Sound Wave Therapy), a unique bio-electronic technology with significant potential. Utilizing the DHSWT program, Dr. Myers is presently concentrating on perfecting a new approach to adult stem cell therapy. Myers' new work is significant in that it is noninvasive, completely benign, and projects the potential of an inexpensive program readily available to all who need it

Dr. Myers currently lives in Clarksville, Tennessee.